There's
No Place
Like Home
for the
Holidays

**OTHER ANTHOLOGIES
EDITED BY SANDRA HALDEMAN MARTZ**

When I Am an Old Woman I Shall Wear Purple

If I Had My Life to Live Over I Would Pick More Daisies

Grow Old Along with Me—The Best Is Yet to Be

Threads of Experience

If I Had a Hammer: Women's Work

I Am Becoming the Woman I've Wanted

There's
No Place
Like Home
for the
Holidays

Edited by
Sandra Haldeman Martz

PAPIER-MACHE PRESS
WATSONVILLE, CA 95076

First Edition

05 04 03 02 01 00 99 98 97   10 9 8 7 6 5 4 3 2 1

ISBN: 1-57601-053-8 Softcover

Cover illustration by Scott Annis
Interior design, interior illustrations, and composition by Elysium
Proofread by Cathey Cordes
Manufactured by Malloy Lithographing, Inc.

Grateful acknowledgment is made to the following publications which first published some of the material in this book: *Israel Horizons*, Vol. 41, No. 2 of 4, Spring/Summer 1993 for "Ram Caught in Thicket" by Karren L. Alenier; *North Coast Review*, Issue #9, Winter 95/96, for "Foreigners" by Marilyn J. Boe; *Houston Chronicle Texas Magazine*, November 24, 1996, for "The One-Sweet-Potato Holiday" by SuzAnne C. Cole; *Chomo-Uri*, 1977, by Barbara Crooker; *Northshore Citizen Newspaper*, Bothell, Washington, December 6, 1995 for "The Search for the Perfect Tree" by Shanna Eilers; *The Grand Rapids Press*, October, 1995, for "The Singing Men of Cleveland" (in a different form) by Linda Nemec Foster; *A Lover's Eye* (The Bunny and The Crocodile Press, Inc., 1989) for "Preparations for Seder" by Michael S. Glaser; *Indianapolis Woman*, December 1984, and *The Village Sampler*, December 1987, for "Holiday Lament" by Shirley Vogler Meister; *Memories of Mama's Kitchens* (Golden Image, 1984) for "Secret Ingredient" by Mary Eileen Price; *The Happy Times Monthly*, Boca Raton, Florida, December 1995, and *The Writers Club*, AOL, November 1996, for "It's New, It's Improved, It's Christmas" by Bob Rhubart; *Homeland* (New Santander Press, 1995) for "It's Time for the Doldrums" by Jan Epton Seale; *Korone*, 1991 and *Slow Miracle* (Lake Shore Publishing, 1992) for "The Day After" by Christine Swanberg; *Antietam Review*, June 1997, for "Waiting for the Pies" by Davi Walders; and *Gloucester Daily Times North Shore Magazine Weekly* for "Card Games" by Suellen Wedmore.

Library of Congress Cataloging-in-Publication Data

There's no place like home for the holidays / edited by Sandra Haldeman Martz.
     p.   cm.
  ISBN 1-57601-053-8 (acid-free, recycled paper)
  1. Family festivals—United States. 2. Holidays—United States. 3. Family festivals—United States—Humor.
  I. Martz, Sandra.
  GT2402.U6T87 1997
  394.26—dc21   97-15678
                                                          CIP

In loving tribute to my sons,
James Van Dyke and John Van Dyke,
and my new daughter,
Tarra McPartland

Contents

Recipes

DESSERTS AND CONFECTIONS

Editor's Preface

Last December my husband and I packed our bags and headed to Yosemite to rendezvous with my in-laws for the holidays. We had reservations for a cozy two-bedroom cabin nestled under snow-covered pines. We'd decided against renting separate cabins since, according to the brochure, some had a fireplace. We pictured the four of us curled up in front of a shared fire, sipping a little Yuletide cheer.

Our first hint of trouble came when we noted the small cabin was marked with two cabin numbers. Entering the door on the left we found one 10 x 12 "two bed" room, a tiny bathroom, an even smaller closet, and almost enough room between the two full-size beds to throw four wet coats. This promised to be family intimacy beyond our wildest imaginations.

Love and a sense of humor prevailed. We organized a schedule for the bathroom, ignored each others' unladylike (ungentlemanly?) noises, ate out a lot, and cut our three-day stay to two days. Moving quickly past the initial disappointment, we agreed that what really mattered was being together. We weren't likely to repeat the adventure, but we couldn't wait to get home and share our outrageous experiences with others.

Back in the office after New Years, I noticed a similar urge among other Papier-Mache folks. Anecdotes entertained and paid homage to our families. Most included vivid descriptions of family members and depicted even the most frustrating events in a humorous light—a safe venting of leftover stress and strain. Without such storytelling, I wondered, would we be as prepared to venture forth the next year?

Our acquisition team began to envision a collection of these stories. We sent a letter to authors we'd published in the past and posted the idea on the internet. Within weeks family anecdotes poured in. To our delight the subject and the submission process drew in some writers we hadn't reached in the past: a fifteen-year-old writer from New York, a ninety-three-year-old newspaper columnist from Ohio, one of our own staff members.

Writers from across the country recalled the joy and madness, the tenderness and exasperation, of dealing with family members against the backdrop of Thanksgiving, Christmas, Passover, and other traditional family get-togethers. Rather than following the calendar, we've let the work flow like a leisurely holiday meal, serving course after course of laughter, poignancy, and appreciation of those rituals and traditions that simultaneously unite us and showcase our uniqueness. There's a dash of healthy cynicism here and there and a gentle reminder that others don't always have families to go home to.

There's also a generous helping of family recipes sprinkled throughout. Try them. They're delicious. Read the stories aloud to your family. Consider it an investment in your own holiday memories. And remember: *There's No Place Like Home for the Holidays.*

—Sandra Haldeman Martz

Home is the place where, when you have to go there,
They have to take you in.

—Robert Frost

Favorite Recipes

Carol Barrett

From an interview by Lin Jakary published in
The Reader, San Diego, April 19, 1984

PLAIN CHICKEN

You get a chicken from Nordstrom's.
Put it in a pan and put some butter on it.
Get some big potatoes. Cut them with a knife.
Put the chicken inside the potatoes.
Put it in the oven for four minutes.
Take it out.
Put it back in for five minutes.
It doesn't cook very good the first time you do it.
—*Ariel Sandler*, Age 3

SPAGHETTI WITH DUCK

Get some ducks. Cut 'em so they can't run.
Throw them in a pan with sugar,
lettuce, and spaghetti noodles.
Don't cook them in water; you have to
cook them in a pan like fried eggs.
Don't put any poison in it.
Eat it with orange juice
and have berry pie for dessert.
—*Rhiannon Morton*, Age 4

BERRY PIE

Go out and pick some berries;
any old berries will do. You have to
drive up to Disneyland to get 'em
'cause you can't find 'em in San Diego.
Make a circle of pie stuff
and pour sugar and berries on top.
Cook it for twenty minutes.
Eat it fast.
—*Rhiannon Morton*, Age 4

FAT STRAWBERRY TURKEY

Get a real turkey from Food Basket;
it should weigh forty-five pounds.
Stuff it with chicken
to make the meat taste like turkey
but leave room for the vegetables.
(I'll tell you about that later.)
—*Sophia Strodtman*, Age 5

TURKEY SAUCE

Smoosh together sugar, salt, potatoes,
and strawberries. The strawberries
are what makes the whole thing
taste good. Now, put the turkey sauce
all over the turkey. Inside of the turkey
you should also put one potato in back
and one potato in front with carrots
in the middle. Put the oven on 450
and cook the whole thing for sixty minutes.
Let it cool off forty-five minutes.
Put toothpicks in it to cool it off faster.
Don't cut off more than you can eat.
—*Sophia Strodtman*, Age 5

Drawing a Pumpkin

Carol Barrett

Sprinkle nutmeg
on your easel. Dip
your pen in fresh
egg yolks and a paste
of honeyed clove. Make
a ground of brown
sugar, a sky of buttermilk,
the leaves stuck to the maples
like cranberry marmalade.
Suck on a stick
of cinnamon and apply
the glaze thick
as eggnog. Hum to yourself
while stirring the cream.

Thanksgiving at My Place

S. Minanel

Relatives sat down to dinner
and praised what was pleasing them most.
For all—the gratitude winner
was not having to be the host!

From the Kitchen of Sheila Kinkead

TURKEY SOUP

Our family really enjoys this soup, and it is a good way to use leftover turkey or chicken. Try it; you will probably like it, and it should not be too fattening.

1 1/2 to 2 cups sliced carrots
1 cup diced celery (optional)
1 medium onion, chopped

In large pot, cover vegetables with water and boil until tender. When vegetables are tender add the following:

1 to 2 cups cooked turkey (or chicken) cut up in bite-sized pieces
Chicken bouillon to taste
Salt and pepper to taste
1 large can or a 12-ounce package of frozen English peas

At this point, you may need to add more water depending upon desired thinness. When the flavors have had time to blend, I add some elbow macaroni or uncooked rice. When the macaroni or the rice is tender, your soup is done.

Eternal Optimist

Charlotte A. Coté

The miles slipped by as we headed due west
three children, a dog, high hopes in my breast—
Christmas was coming, with promises made,
but hopes they'd be kept had started to fade.

As each rest stop sign loomed up by the road
the squeals and the kicks grew ever more bold.
The dog frisked about and barked in high glee
each time we slowed down and soon I could see

our four-hour trip would soon stretch to six
as the children began to try their pet tricks.
I muffled my ears against their shrill cries
turned to my husband who just closed his eyes.

I knew this meant he was quitting the race
'twas up to me now to keep up the pace.
"Home for the holidays," I said so low
the children stopped talking. "So why do we go

to see all these folks we don't know any more,
friends, aunts and uncles, and cousins galore?
Why do we do it?" I asked loud and clear
and a voice from the back fell on my ear.

"'Cause they're our family; you grew up with them."
Such words of wisdom I could not condemn.
I laughed and I shouted, "Let's be on our way.
We want to get there while it's still to*day*."

I stepped on the gas, the wheels spun around,
we flew down the road with hardly a sound.
The children grew quiet, then fell fast asleep,
the dog stretched out sweetly and made not a peep.

We pulled up at Grandma's at quarter past three,
in plenty of time to set up the tree,
piled presents beneath it and then turned to find
my brother arriving, his family behind.

His very first words were, "Where can I park?"
as though this whole thing was just a big lark.
While Grandpa rushed out to help the new crew
I dashed upstairs for I instantly knew

I must claim a bedroom. Now I could see
if I didn't act fast, on the floor I would be.
Upstairs and downstairs the children did run
to see where they'd sleep, to stir up some fun.

I spread out the luggage across the big bed
pulled out my slippers, and down the stairs fled
straight to the kitchen where the work had increased,
I started some pies for the big Christmas feast.

The children were fed and sent off to bed
Grandpa just chuckled and shook his grey head.
We worked in the kitchen till late in the night,
the turkey and trimmings would be a delight.

The stuffing was ready, the yams were all done
and now I looked forward to having some fun
but two of the children were sick until four.
By dawn the next morning they'd opened the door

shouting, "It's Christmas, let's open the presents!"
How could I spoil one of life's greatest moments?
Soon paper and ribbon littered the floor;
the children jumped up and looked round for more.

I asked them to gather all boxes and trash
before they could eat, and they flew like a flash
grabbed everything up and took it outside
while Grandma looked on, smiling with pride.

More family showed up—the fun really started
as we tried our best to keep children parted,
sent little ones downstairs to whoop and to play
middle ones to the den, told them to stay.

The oldest we thought could help set the table
but soon found them all, unwilling, unable.
They managed somehow to break a big plate
chipped up another so we thought we'd not wait

for more broken dishes. We sent them outside
to go for a walk or take a long ride
on the bikes that Grandpa set out from the shed
with the help of husband and good Uncle Ned

leaving Grandma, Aunt Milly, sweet sister Sue,
dear cousin Agnes, sister-in-law too
to put our great feast on the table by one
to round up the children and seat everyone.

So there'd be no squabbling, each child was to sit
beside an adult (we all thought it fit)
to oversee helpings and stop any spills
but it didn't take long for a loud clash of wills:

who gets a drumstick, who gets a wing,
who hates potatoes, who hates everything,
who wants to get down and run out and play
who will insist on ruining the day.

No promise of pie or even ice cream
could settle the matter now it would seem.
We could send all the toys back to the North Pole
but they were intent on a much better goal:

playing with Johnny's new tractor and plow,
meal interrupted, we settled the row.
And so it all goes for the rest of the day
ignoring the children, we eat, drink, and weigh

the thought of gathering again next year.
But Grandma just smiles—she holds us all dear—

and Grandpa is beaming, proud as can be;
children, grandchildren, we're his family.

So it looks like we'll continue to drive,
Home for the Holidays! Home to the Hive!

From the Kitchen of Charlotte Coté

MASHED POTATO PATTIES

Lots of mashed potatoes left over after a big holiday dinner? A simple and delicious solution:

Sauté finely chopped onion in margarine or butter until translucent (about one teaspoon per patty). Mix into leftover mashed potatoes along with a dash of garlic powder, summer savory, salt, and pepper. Brown patties in oil or margarine until crisp on both sides. Serve hot.

Home is not where you live
but where they understand you.

—Christian Morgenstern

The Call

Julia Fisher

This past Christmas season, I kept getting call after call from friends who were sad or crying. Their mothers were being jerks, their siblings were being asses, their fathers never change, etc., etc., etc. I, on the other hand, had known better and had stayed *away* from my family for the holidays.

Halfway through the umpteenth call, I had an idea: I told the friend on the other end of the line that I was starting a not-for-profit group called Dysfunctional Families of America, based on the model of Alcoholics Anonymous. The idea, I told her, was this: "The next time you get the urge to call or to visit 'them,' call me first, and I will talk you out of it!" Well, my friend laughed and laughed. And so did each person thereafter who called with her (always *her!*) story of family woe.

Godiva Chocolates

Melissa Milich

"Promise me," I told Greg, "we'll go back the day after Christmas." We were about to get into the car for an eleven hour round-trip to visit his side of the family. They had the monopoly on Christmas. I had an application for a graduate program due a few days after Christmas, and I still had a lot of work to do on it. Greg was on a deadline himself, and said, "No problem. We'll go back the next morning."

"Promise," I said.

"Promise," he said.

I've always wondered who are the scrooges who decide applications for graduate school are due January 1. Don't the application committees understand such things as Christmas nightmares? It's always a nightmare because we have to go to Greg's parents in Los Angeles. The men go off into the den by themselves and watch football, and the women are expected to stay together and talk about diets. I hate to talk about diets. His aunt gave me a pair of control top panty hose one year for Christmas if that gives you any idea why I hate to talk about diets.

And speaking of the perfect present, not only do we have to buy just the perfect presents for all his cousins and aunts and interlopers who we see only once a year anyway, but the wrapping paper has to be *just right*. Greg and I got in a big fight before we left on our trip because I thought I had more wrapping paper in the closet than I did—it was dark in the closet and it *felt* like Christmas paper, but when Greg pulled it out later, it was Valentine's Day paper with big BE MINE hearts on it, and I said while Greg was starting to steam, "Hey! It'll be funny!"

His family doesn't have the Milich warped sense of humor, so I offered to let Greg use the comic pages from that morning's Sunday paper even though I hadn't finished reading them—Hey, our family always wraps presents in the funny papers.

We bought wrapping paper on our way to Los Angeles, and I managed to wrap fourteen presents in a moving car. It was valuable time that I could have spent instead thinking about my graduate school application. But there I was twisting and turning in a Volkswagen Bug, trying to wrap the packages for his family *just right* while Greg was driving seventy miles an hour trying to guarantee we'd get there on time. His mother actually checks to make sure the wrapping on the presents is folded into hospital corners. "Oh my," she'll say, "this one isn't wrapped very well."

Right about when we came to Santa Barbara, the point in our journey where there's no turning back, when I had Scotch tape in my hair, and I had cut my fingers on the scissors trying to curl the ribbon, I repeated the mantra that would get me through the next thirty-six hours: *"Promise me we'll come back the day after Christmas."*

"I promise," he said.

So what happened? On Christmas day we were all at Greg's aunt's house in our stiff Christmas outfits—suits, ties, festive dresses, and high heels—sitting on white couches, taking dainty bites out of Godiva chocolates and there was a lull in the merriment and promises forgotten, when suddenly Greg's mother said—she is the matriarch of the family—"When are you going back?"

The room stopped and all the cousins and aunts and interlopers looked at us and Greg's mother said, "I think you should go spend a few days in Lake Forest with your second removed cousin and his gorgeous wife," and Greg, I'll kill him one of these days, looked at me and said, "Well, it's up to her. She's the one that has to get back."

So the whole room was focused on me and not because I had Godiva chocolate dotting the corners of my mouth, but because suddenly the whole unity of Greg's family depended upon me: the happiness of the rest of the day, the entire Christmas holiday, whether Greg's cousin's marriage would hold together, whether the members sitting there with their mouths open would be able to keep their New Year's resolutions, and the promise of Peace for the next twenty years into the Millennium, it all depended upon me.

"I think I have to go back tomorrow."

I tried to say this in a tiny, tiny voice, hoping the family might hear what they wanted to hear, that afterward I could drag Greg into a dark corner and beat him up, and we could sneak out the next morning while an uncle was making scrambled eggs for breakfast and the female cousins were getting ready to go to the After Christmas Sales. But that's not what happened. I won't tell you about all the shouts of dismay. I won't go into detail about how I felt that I wrecked Christmas. I will tell you we returned home by midnight the next day, and I got my graduate school application in, including the essay portion, "Why I Want to Go to Stanford." Somehow I wrote something halfway intelligent, an interesting piece on prima donna writers and horse manure. Really. One gets very creative on deadline.

Then I sat down and wrote thank-you notes to all Greg's cousins and aunts. I had stolen some Godiva chocolates from their stash before we left, slipping them into my purse. I finished them off while I wrote the cousins and aunts, thanking them for the control top panty hose, that this particular brand of panty hose was doing a lot to control my figure, plus you don't feel like having second helpings when they're pinching your waistline so tightly! And that I looked forward to spending Christmas with them next year . . .

Holiday Lament

Shirley Vogler Meister

Oh, my heavens! Can it be
the holidays crept up on me?
Time is fleeting; I'm in panic
rush, rush, rushing like a manic.
Much too busy to collapse,
I count the days—then I lapse
into depression, deep and bleak.
Can I be the only freak
who's frowning while all others smile
their greetings in such happy style?
"What's so wrong?" the family asks,
minimizing all my tasks.
Then from all sides I'm advised:
"For goodness sakes, get organized!"

From the Kitchen of Jo Gregory

MAMA'S ANGEL BISCUITS

5 cups flour
1 teaspoon soda
3 teaspoons baking powder
1 tablespoon salt
1 package dry yeast dissolved in 1/2 cup warm water
3/4 cup shortening
2 cups buttermilk
3 tablespoons sugar

Sift dry ingredients together. Cut in shortening until the flour makes little pea-like balls (similar to making pie crust). Add the yeast mixture, buttermilk, and sugar to make a soft dough. Knead on a floured board until dough is elastic. Cut out biscuits with a cookie cutter (or an 8-ounce empty can with the bottom and top cut out). Let sit for 10 minutes. Bake at 450 degrees F for 10 to 15 minutes.

Foreigners

Marilyn J. Boe

I need to take a nap to shorten my day,
as I did in Norway, when relatives hurried
toward me, Norwegian tumbling, while I
fumbled for my dictionary; the few phrases
I'd practiced called out to be corrected.

I'm language weary today in my own home,
this holiday season,
surrounded by foreigners; grown children
who visit, decide to rearrange furniture,
sweep my house clear of books,
papers, unclutter my tables like a model home.
They tell me I need "horizontal lines,"
as if I were a train without a track,
but their area downstairs rises higher each day
with mounds of wet towels, dirty clothes,
and I must guide the gas man
to the meter through a maze of apologies.

All the words in my Mother Dictionary
have been used up and the smile they give me
is the smile natives beam onto a foreigner
who chatters on and on, thinking
she's being understood.

Six Grown Kids
Back Home for Christmas

Lorraine Tolliver

We are a six-headed Hydra.
One jabs, two jokes,
three stings, four strokes,
five digs, six ducks.

One is gentle, two benign,
three is sassy, four unkind,
five spouts detail hour on hour,
six sprinkles platitudes' numbing power.

One jumps ahead leap by leap,
two is puffed up in silent retreat,
three puts on the robe of king,
four rebels and takes to wing,
five whimpers and begs for pity,
six is best being sharp and witty.

We're a peculiar bundle of nerves and knuckles,
all strapped together by a tight belt and buckle
and doing an improvised dance in a circle.

Ram Caught in Thicket

Karren L. Alenier

Great Uncle Sidney (read Abraham)
as the allegation goes, clobbered
his son Michael (substitute Isaac)
with a leg of lamb, perversion
of the legendary knife used
at the first circumcision. Maybe
it was Passover and Michael romped
under elbow, helping his klutzy
father who let bone and wobbly flesh
slip through his hand, smack
his surprised offspring, grease
the boy's crewcut like no barber
ever would. Maybe it happened later
at the Crossroads, a grill Uncle
owned in the '50s on the old route
to Baltimore. Say it was the dinner
hour and besides the regular clientele,
his brother's family—Sol, Etta, their
gaggle of girls and one lonely son—
dropped by. An acne'd Michael slammed
into the kitchen calling, "Dad!"
to which Sidney boomed, "Here am I!"
Followed by son exclaiming he was
headed to the drive-in with a girl named Mary Beth.
"What about Rebekah, your cousin's, dinner?"

This an irate father fumed and swiveled
with the leg of meat, his fingers leached
white and oof, the collision. "Why me?
What did I do?" still burned, Michael,
years later, yells at his father.

The story simmers like stew. What the burnt
offering was, only God knows.

From the Kitchen of Sadie Block

SADIE'S NOODLE KUGEL

This dish should not be served at Passover because of the noodles. (Potato kugel is served at Passover.)

1-pound package of wide noodles
2 eggs, well beaten
1/2 to 3/4 large carton cottage cheese
1/2 small carton sour cream
1/2 cube margarine, melted
Apple, peeled and cut into chunks
Raisins
Pinch of salt
Few shakes of cinnamon
Pinch of nutmeg

Boil noodles in salted water and drain. Mix all other ingredients in ovenproof dish which has been buttered first, and bake at 375 degrees F for 45 minutes.

Passover's Last Stand

Gail Pickus

My good friend Susie calls tonight. Since the snow dropped its extraordinary load on our little midwestern town this winter, we've all tried to escape to more ambient spots. Even though Susie's in California and I'm in Texas, we haven't given up our need to talk about things as usual. It's close friendships that make living in our small town so endearing. We are in and out of each others' houses and love knowing whole generations in a family and all the family stories that go with them. "Do you remember my telling you the story about our last Passover supper?" she asks.

Of course I do! It is one of my favorite Passover stories. Seasonally, Passover is the traditional time of year when Jewish families gather together all the generations for a long and sumptuous meal, following the reading of the proscribed story of the Exodus from Egypt, and the eating of symbolic foods. It was at this gathering and at this table at this time of the year that Susie and Jack and their three boys welcomed their large and multigenerational family to join them. And so they sat amidst the sparkling goblets of wine, the Seder plate, and the heaping platters of delicious, specially prepared Passover food.

Among the cast of characters seated at the table were Jack's father, Abe, and his second wife, Esther. Abe, a successful store owner and politician, now retired, was a distinguished white-mustachioed gentleman, imposing in strength, but very hard of hearing; Esther was a bit of a ditz who practiced self-hypnosis for painless trips to the dentist's office and claimed to know famous folk we could only wonder about. This name-dropping intimidated Susie's mother, Patsy, sitting across the table from Esther. Patsy ordinarily loved zapping back across the table, but this time she was partially distracted by her brother Bush, sitting next to her, who had been sprung from the nursing home for this special family dinner. Bush must have been on medication because he kept falling asleep, his head lolling into his full dinner plate. Patsy would carefully lift his head from the plate and admonish, "Wipe your nose, Bush!"

Abe would then ask, "What did she say?" And around the table the reply would go—"She said 'Wipe your nose, Bush!'"—from Susie and Jack's three boys all the way around to Abe's sister, Esta, who was sitting on Bush's other side.

"Oh," he said, mollified at last, and then turned to continue the argument he was having with Esta about the correct year their father had come to this country. Tall angular Esta was vigorously argumentative and responsible for the constant undertone of bickering at the table. Gesturing dramatically with her large hands, Esta sat enthroned in her black cape, head crooked at an angle, big eyes wide with intensity as she delivered to Abe the true dates their parents had bought and sold the store. This insidious undercurrent had not gone unnoticed.

By this time, Jack and Susie at either end of the table could hardly contain themselves. Accidentally making eye contact and afraid of bursting into laughter right there at the table, they excused themselves, tore into the family room, and fell on the floor, dissolved in laughter. Whereupon their oldest son, Mike, appeared, hands on hips, a disapproving look on his face.

"What do you think you're doing?" he remonstrated.

"You don't think this is funny?" They could hardly believe he'd missed the hilarity of the scene at the dinner table and all its components. Susie gave up. She said, "This is the last family Passover dinner we're going to have in this house for a long time."

So now, years later, Susie reminds me of that infamous dinner. "Well," she says, "we have become the lead players in that story." She and Jack and their nephew, Gary, have just had dinner in a noisy California restaurant. Susie has laryngitis and can hardly speak. Jack is now somewhat hard of hearing. As Gary sat between them, trying to translate their conversations back and forth, she and Jack howled with laughter that the tables had been turned on them after all those years. Susie says it's all pretty scary. I say it makes a wonderful end to the story of the Last Passover Supper.

The Day After

Christine Swanberg

Today I celebrate glorious nothing,
put my phone on cruise control
so no one can intrude upon my uncelebration.

Today is my true Sabbath,
a day when I am free to unplug
work, family, shopping, feast.

This day once was the blue pine
of too much everything too sweet
and stale, a tally of cookies,

relatives who say all the wrong things,
a day for crying over what has never been
and what will never be. But today

I claim nothing
but this good cup of coffee,
streak of blue in the skylight,

a frost terrarium of ferns,
conifers and feathers,
this old pen and used paper,

my good old ass
anchored in this chair, and just
hang out in this slow miracle.

Peace Unearthed

Deborah Shouse

My daughter Sarah and I live alone now. Our house is quiet and contemplative. I come home from work and slip down into the newspaper; my daughter comes home from school and slides into the television. She irons out her mind with talk shows—I unwind my brain with crossword puzzles. Some evenings, we throw together a quick dinner; other evenings, she has basketball, art classes, dinner with friends. I have seminars, work, dinner with friends. We are a serene civilized household, our voices melodious and calm, our interactions poised and possessed. We write notes detailing practical matters. "Could you get me washer fluid?" she writes. "Could you put the dirty dishes in the dishwasher?" I write. We sign our memos with smiling faces and hearts.

Tonight, I come home from work and the house is bulging, belching, and guffawing. Our refuge has been commandeered by four wild men and one wise woman: my family is visiting for the holidays.

My kitchen is now a morass of floor toys, spilled spices, crusty pots.

"We're cooking from scratch," my brother explains.

Sarah and I are used to spaces between people, pauses between sentences, room to stretch. My family crowds into the kitchen, creating a stew of advice, demands, and interjections.

"I'm thirsty," my six-year-old nephew Jacob announces, and promptly spills half his milk while sliding sock-footed on the floor.

"I want to help," his older brother Zach says. He sits on a cluttered counter and spreads out cards for a game of solitaire.

My brother instructs me: "Chop onions, slice mushrooms, peel carrots, then sauté." I obey.

Sarah sits tearing lettuce. Her friend Jenny appears and peels a couple of apples.

Gradually the floor gathers flour, splats of butter, scraps of apple peel. Somehow Jacob's Batman falls into the pie dough. Somehow the paper towels get loose from their prissy roll and create an inviting path along the floor.

"Have you heard the one about the farmer?" my father says, and we all groan. My mother stoops on the floor with a damp cloth, trying to keep things clean.
Sarah and Jenny graze along the stove, dipping into the gravy, nipping into the carrots, sampling just one mushroom.

Jacob vrooms back and forth, Batman warring with the Transformer. Zach, bored with his cards, seizes the Transformer and Jacob punches him.

"He hit me!" Zach yells.

"He took my transformer!" Jacob shouts.

"Shhh, I'm telling a joke," my father says.

"Boys, slow down," my mother cautions.

"Zach, Jacob," my brother warns, his voice fierce.

Our kitchen is used to soothing sounds and polite conversation. Sarah and I are queens of calm, a sisterhood of manners.

As Jacob zooms past me, I remember what it was like when my daughters were younger: the constant hands reaching and wanting, the unpaved road of chatter and quarreling, the never ending nearness.

Sarah comes over to pick an onion out of the stir fry.

"Boys sure are noisy," she whispers.

I smile, remembering how very noisy she used to be.

"I bet you haven't heard this one," my father says and begins a story about a man and a dry cleaner's.

"Not again, I've heard this one too many times," my mother complains.

The grease sputters, and Jacob shouts, "I'm thirsty."

My brother puts another pot on the stove and nudges me.

"Are you paying attention to your cooking?" he teases.

Zach launches into a comedy routine from *Saturday Night Live*. My father begins another joke. Jacob turns into a human airplane.

I look around the crowded kitchen.

"Isn't it amazing we can all be in the same room and get along?" I say.

Only my mother hears. She nods.

I close my eyes and listen to the roller coaster decibel of voices, the sudden shrieks, and then bubbling laughter. The sounds are a medley I'd forgotten, a familiar poignant tune.

This clamoring and chaos is the essence of my family, and I realize how much I have longed to hear it. Underneath the noise and nattering, the crying and confusion, I feel a sense of deep connectedness and of peace, unearthed.

Home is where the heart is.

—Pliny the Elder

A Time for Giving Thanks

Therese Tappouni

And so it is. In our family, time for three generations, going on four, to brush up on their latest charade titles. There are those of us who are fiercely competitive, those who try to get four-year-olds in the game, and those who watch, quivering with insecurity, from the sidelines. And there's my husband, who has manned the clock for years. His background being foreign to the American sense of fun, he has chosen to not expose himself to the ridiculous and sublime tradition of Thanksgiving Day charades. For some unknown reason, on this particular afternoon, he came off the bench.

As usual, we had eaten a dual meal of turkey, stuffing, oysters, and pumpkin pie for the German/Irish/American side of the clan, and a buffet of kibbe, stuffed grape leaves, and baklava for the Mideast contingent. How we had energy for this high-spirited competition year after year when we were stuffed like the Easter lamb was something we never contemplated. It would not have been Thanksgiving without thirty-plus people in the family room pulling on their ears and bugging their eyes out as if to say, "What can you be thinking? It's so *obvious!*" The highlight so far had been my mother, in her seventies, leaping from a living room chair, arms outspread, and wondering why we didn't guess Willie Nelson's "Angel Flying Too Close to the Ground." When the teenagers inserted titles, the adults turned pink but gamely persisted. And when the older generation put the "Beer Barrel Polka" in the bowl, the kids already had a set piece for it. It had reappeared for the past ten years, after all.

On the particular year I speak of, tragedy had been a companion to my sister's husband. Following a nearly fatal car accident, he had diligently struggled to retain his balance, his language, and his self-respect. When he said, "I'm in," my husband came forward and whispered, "Me too," as if he were hoping no one would hear him. But they did. The kids and grandkids were astounded. Uncle Joe and Uncle Mike, on the same team. Did we have the heart to work against them with our superior mobility and craft? It was a challenge to our competitive instincts and our generosity of spirit. Everyone waited, barely breathing, as the team including Joe and Mike drew first. Mike, the immigrant who had never played, stood tall in the center of the room and slowly unfolded his paper. He studied it for what seemed an eternity, emotions flying across his face, his legs quivering as if that last piece of pie in the kitchen was calling him. Anywhere but here, was what his face cried out.

I wondered if we had made a major mistake. Joe's reasoning abilities were slow, Mike was a deer in the headlights. How could this possibly be a good thing? The rest of their team was a daughter who was good at giving clues and a host of kids, some of them experiencing their first charades experience, like Mike. I felt such compassion as he slowly folded the paper and neatly stuck it in his pants pocket. One more time, he pulled it out and reread it. I groaned. It must be one of those long clues, or the ever popular "Inabagadavita," or whatever the heck that perennial flower child entry was. Back into the pocket the clue went, and my dignified, old-country husband settled on the balls of his feet, looked around his team, took a deep breath, and went over the edge. It was worse than I could have imagined. He pulled open his shirt, literally popping the buttons, and was pounding on his chest and yelling into the room. We sat, stunned into incomprehension, but it wasn't over. Joe leapt to his feet brandishing his cane.

"Conan the Barbarian!" he yelled, his voice bouncing from the back wall, his feet threatening to go out from under him. His eyes met the eyes of my husband as the echo of his voice slid into the corners of the room, into the silence of the family, lost on the inhaled breaths of adults and the delighted yelps of the little ones. And then, my husband smiled. He reached delicately into his pocket, brought out the folded paper, unfolded it, and showed it to the room. There, in the block letters printed by one of the younger cousins, was MOVIE: CONAN THE BARBARIAN.

The sounds of a sighing wind grew as everyone took a breath and my mother, the timer for the group this particular year, said into the breeze, "It's a family record. Two seconds." My husband and my brother-in-law had twin grins splitting their faces as they pounded on their chests, aging Arnold Schwarzeneggers who had beaten the odds and produced a miracle, all because the time was right.

From the Kitchen of Therese Tappouni

TURKEY SALAD

2 cups cubed leftover turkey (preferably white meat)

1 stalk celery, minced

1 green onion, minced

1/2 cup white grapes, sliced in half

1 teaspoon orange juice (optional)

3 tablespoons mayonnaise (or salad dressing)

Salt and pepper to taste

Mix and serve on tomatoes as a salad or on bread as sandwiches.

Thanksgiving

Barbara Crooker

Grey clouds knit the mountains,
the ceilings lower,
as the dough in the oven rises and swells.
Risen at dawn, my mother fixes stuffing,
adds a pinch of sage, not rosemary,
remembering her mother's recipe.
She trusses the bird, plump and naked,
rubs it with butter, skewers it shut.

This is the longest day of the year.
The mantle clock drips out minutes,
the coffee brews; we wait all day to eat.
Football games crackle in the den;
men talk statistics,
there is safety in numbers.

Back in the kitchen, we line up the pies:
apple, pecan, mince. Sweat beads
on the rim of the pumpkin.
We speak in recipes,
measuring our replies.

Then the timer buzzes,
the pressure cooker rocks,
and frantically
we spice, carve, and mash.

Stuffed with memories, we nibble at talk,
pick gingerly around the old scabs.
We are polite, we only break bread.
I praise the creamed onions.
"Anyone for leftovers?" my mother asks,
shaking the foil. Pass the mints.
We have come through another year.

From the Kitchen of Barbara Crooker

AUNT MARSHA'S RECIPE
FOR THE DAY AFTER THANKSGIVING
Take turkey carcass; throw it in the garbage.
Check out all the flyers; shop till you drop.
It's Black Friday; let the Christmas season begin!
Order a takeout pizza, put your feet up, and relax.

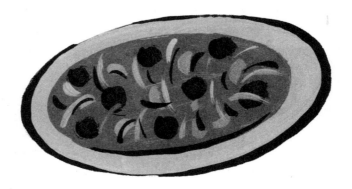

Return for the Holiday

Marsha Rogers

Sometimes you have to kick them out.
    She'll die a wrinkled old virgin!
Some go willingly,
    You idiot! Did you miss something?
others are forced.
    She's married.
For some reason
    Who's she seeing now?
they always come back.
    Fred-Fred-Bill-Fred.
The impromptu gathering of the clan
was the first in over a year.
    No way.
Time had been needed
    Never have sex to music,
for healing the rift.
    it screws the rhythm.
The youngest and oldest
    What are you doing with my son?
led the way.
    Corrupting him? Good!
New and old flowed together
    Yes! Go for it, Mom!
like no time had passed.

From the Kitchen of Kelly J. Hughes

TURKEY AND CHEESE ENCHILADAS

6 large flour tortillas
2 cups shredded, cooked turkey
3 cups shredded Monterey Jack cheese
6 tablespoons chopped green onion
1/4 cup margarine
1/4 cup flour
2 cups chicken broth
1 cup sour cream
1 (4-ounce) can green chiles, seeded and chopped

Fill each tortilla with 1/3 cup turkey, 1/2 cup cheese, and 1 tablespoon green onion. Roll each tortilla and place in a 9 x 13-inch baking dish. Melt margarine in a medium-size saucepan over medium heat. Add flour, stirring constantly until smooth. Add chicken broth, stirring constantly, to make a thick sauce. Remove from heat and add sour cream and chiles; stir until smooth. Pour sauce over tortillas. If desired, top enchiladas with additional shredded cheese and chopped green onion. Bake at 350 degrees F for 20 minutes until heated through.

Once More with Stuffing

Meg Huber

Every year we say, "Let's *really* have a gathering for Thanksgiving," and every year our second thought is, "Here comes trouble." But we love Thanksgiving dinners so each year I cook three of them. The first is a small private dinner with just our children. One child is disabled and needs to have his dinner served to him midday. The second Thanksgiving dinner is held the night of the official day and is served to reward a brother's kin for spending eleven hours on the road while we were eating meal one. Why I serve the third dinner I cannot say, but while smarter women are getting a jump on Christmas shopping, our tradition is to invite people from other countries to dinner. Perhaps all that pumpkin pie and stuffing on Thursday unleashes unexpected energy because one never knows what will happen on Thanksgiving Friday.

Enter the guests. One holds us in uneasy thrall explaining the logic of government-sponsored single-child families in China. We look around the room. Only one among us is a first child. Next a guest from the Ukraine brings the conversation to an uneasy pause by suggesting that one way to deal with Third World nations is to let them all starve. On this note, I call folks to the table. As we sit down, Grandma, who is visiting from Florida, mistakes a nine-year-old girl in overalls for a boy. Next, Grandma loudly requests that someone please remove the stuffed cabbages from her end of the table. Fortunately, the Russian cabbage cook is so close to drowning in the sea of English that she just smiles and isn't offended.

Just then an air inversion pulls heavy smoke from the fireplace over to our table. Windows and doors, stripped of their screens the previous week, fly open, and the indoor cat sees his moment to escape. The cook flies to the fireplace to monkey with the damper, succeeding in closing it completely. By now the smoke is oppressive, and one guest, having driven eleven hours, is sure he is getting a headache so it is on with the attic fan. One young woman quietly retrieves her red wool coat from the closet and pulls it over Grandma's legs to keep her warm. A few moments of artificial wind through the house clears the smoke. We close the windows, put on coffee, and check out Grandma, resplendent in her coat-blanket, smiling at the lot of us. It seems the best Thanksgiving ever, we agree. Maybe it is all that stuffing and pumpkin pie.

Absence is one of the most useful ingredients of family life, and to do it rightly is an art like any other.

—Freya Stark

The One-Sweet-Potato Holiday

SuzAnne C. Cole

The first call came at the end of October. Our middle son had decided he wouldn't try to come home for Thanksgiving from college—too many papers due and California was too far away. However, he'd already been asked to join a friend's family for dinner, so we shouldn't worry; he wouldn't be lonely.

In early November our oldest son called. His wife's brother, whom she hadn't seen since their August wedding, was going to be in New York for Thanksgiving, so would it be all right if they spent the holiday with him instead of coming to Texas to spend it with us? Of course, we said, knowing Elisabeth had been homesick for her French family.

Later that month when our youngest son decided it wasn't worth two days of travel from his Vermont college to spend two days with us for Thanksgiving, we weren't too disappointed. After all, we still expected my parents and sister for the holiday. And then my mother called: "Honey, I'm sorry, but the doctor just told your dad absolutely no travel for the next few months. Could you come to Oklahoma?" After briefly considering the twenty-hour round trip for a four-day holiday, I reluctantly said we couldn't.

So in the chilly afternoon light that Thanksgiving Eve, my husband and I loaded up our car and our old dog and left Houston for New Braunfels and our first Thanksgiving alone as a couple—ever. What would that feel like for us? When his parents were alive, Thanksgiving had always been their holiday with us, usually at our condo in New Braunfels. After their deaths, we had continued the ritual of spending Thanksgiving there, but always with some of our family around. Accustomed to the traditional feast and family visiting, would we be desolate?

With none of the usual holiday preparation to do the night before, I slept ten hours. Thanksgiving dawned bright and cold. We spent the morning inside by the fire in self-indulgence: I read through months of magazines and journals while my husband watched the Oilers.

Early in the afternoon, just an hour or so before we intended to eat, I went into the kitchen to start dinner. I remembered other years when I had arisen at dawn to make stuffing, prepare the turkey for roasting, roll out pie dough, and set the table, sitting down for the first time when we ate and finding myself too tired to really taste the food. So I wasn't really sorry to be making dinner for two instead of eight—or eighteen.

Feeling hungry, my husband wandered into the kitchen and saw a single yam sitting on the counter. With a look of mingled surprise and regret, he asked wistfully, "Only one sweet potato?" I knew he was recalling other Thanksgivings: hot, steamy kitchens fragrant with cloves and butter and roasting turkey, every horizontal surface covered with delicious dishes the womenfolk were preparing. As I hugged him, I too remembered the ritual of Thanksgiving in my childhood.

At my grandparents' Kansas farm there were always enough aunts, uncles, and cousins in attendance to set at least two tables—children ritually segregated from grownups, starched embroidered cloths centered with autumn leaves and pinecone and paper-bag turkeys. Grandmother Mary would serve an enormous turkey oozing juice from its golden cracking skin, pans of giblet dressing baked crispy on the top, moist and steamy inside, candied sweet potatoes topped with melting marshmallows, pork roast and a platter of chicken for those who didn't like turkey, yeast rolls, cinnamon-flecked applesauce, pickled peaches studded with cloves, creamed corn, green beans cooked with bacon, white potatoes whipped into peaks and gilded with butter, and a cut crystal bowl of ambrosia, all of this washed down with milk and tea. Later there would be pie— mince and pumpkin, of course, but also cherry and peach—a coconut-topped layer cake, plates of black walnut cookies, and my grandfather's favorite chocolate-covered cherries. And lots of storytelling and reminiscing as we sat pushed back from the table, somnolent and stuffed.

Now I turned to my husband and said, "It's a Texas-sized potato—and besides, neither one of us really likes sweet potatoes that much." We went back to the fire and had a glass of champagne and pâté with crackers while I set the table with our usual dishes and silverware and the decorative items I had brought from Houston—a folk art pilgrim couple, a small bouquet of flowers, and some turkey paper napkins. We sat down, blessed our food and our absent families, and talked about how grateful we were for what we had accomplished as parents. We congratulated ourselves that this new ritual of spending a holiday alone was proof that we had given our children permission to lead their own independent lives.

We ate the simple meal—a small honey-glazed turkey breast, wild rice, broccoli, green beans, and that solitary baked sweet potato—and shared a nice bottle of chardonnay. Dessert was a pumpkin cheesecake from our favorite bakery. Cleaning up the kitchen took ten minutes followed by a long nap. I didn't miss the hours the women spent working to restore order in Grandmother's kitchen after the holiday meal.

We spent the rest of the weekend doing as we pleased. We talked about retirement and the children and our jobs for hours. We shopped, we saw a movie, my husband played golf, I read and wrote. One sunny afternoon we walked through Landa Park, numbing our fingers in Comal Springs and talking about what the Founder's Oak, a majestic live oak thought to have been growing since 1700, had witnessed. At the end of three days we returned to Houston, refreshed, restored, and mellowed by intimacy unencumbered with the usual holiday chores and responsibilities.

We've had two more one-sweet-potato Thanksgivings since that first one; the menu changes from year to year, but one sweet potato remains a staple, the symbol for a holiday alone. Perhaps one day we will again have a house full of people for Thanksgiving, and I will happily polish silver, iron linens, plan menus, and cook for days. Or perhaps not. Spending a holiday as a family of two, we learned not to mourn what we didn't have, but instead to relish what we did have—solitude and time together.

From the Kitchen of
Sandra Martz

GOOD TO THE LAST BITE SWEET POTATO SOUFFLÉ

2 cups mashed sweet potatoes (or yams)
4 tablespoons melted butter
4 tablespoons brandy
1/2 cup light cream
4 eggs
1/2 teaspoon salt
1 teaspoon grated lemon rind
1/4 teaspoon nutmeg
1/2 teaspoon cinnamon
1/4 teaspoon mace

Beat sweet potatoes, butter, brandy, cream, salt, lemon rind, and spices until well blended. Beat egg yolks until stiff and lemony colored. Fold into sweet potato mixture. Beat egg whites until stiff. Fold into sweet potato mixture. Pour into buttered baking dish (approximately one quart size). Bake 25 minutes at 375 degrees F. Makes six servings.

Garbanzo Beans

Karen Ackland

One Thanksgiving several years ago my best friend spent most of the dinner arguing with her boyfriend about pumpkin pies. One felt they were better made with evaporated milk; the other insisted on half-and-half. The rest of us could only call on the authority of our own families and no one conceded the argument. This seemed to confirm the anthropological theory that you can tell a tribe by what they eat. This Christmas I was merging two tribes. My husband's parents and his two daughters, Danielle and Jennifer, were coming to stay for a week.

Last March I had committed an act of optimism and remarried in middle age. I was not a reluctant bride, but being married pleased me more than I expected and for eight months I was dumb in a private happiness. Then my husband had a major project due and started working fifteen hours a day. And I started anticipating Christmas.

Christmas did not seem to be bringing out the best in me. For years I thought that I didn't like Christmas because I was single. Every year I went home to my parents where I would be treated kindly like some overgrown child who was watched surreptitiously to see if I would drink too much or mention something they'd rather not know. I had no status as a single person and had to share a room with my sister's children. But now I was respectfully married. I had a husband, two stepchildren, a Christmas tree, and I was still looking forward to January.

My family's holiday tradition is trying new recipes. Before an upcoming holiday my father and I get out cookbooks, torn pages from the newspaper, the holiday issues of *Sunset* and *Gourmet* magazines, and read recipes out loud to each other. My mother makes suggestions, but her main role is saying, "Do you know how expensive that will be?" The room is filled with possibilities. The almond macaroon dressing with pomegranate seeds. The pears poached in merlot. The cranberry sauce with garlic and ginger. We end up with enough recipes for five dinners and go through a final elimination round, making sure there is enough color in the meal. Plate presentation is very important to my father.

My husband is not a cook and does not share this interest in recipes. He tries to look attentive as I spread out the cookbooks on the kitchen table for the fourth night in a row, but these questions are making him irritable. I know that but, like trying to convince someone of the virtues of half-and-half, I can't believe that he won't eventually find this satisfying. The quieter he gets, the more I try to engage him in conversation.

"What are your family's traditions? Should I make something special?"

"I can't think of anything."

"What about the potatoes?" I know people have strong feelings about potatoes. "Do you think they'd like them mashed with garlic? Or sweet potatoes? There is a nice au gratin recipe in here with sweet potatoes."

"You are getting uptight," my husband announces unhelpfully.

Of course I am uptight. I am trying to plan a Christmas celebration for five people from an alien tribe. The last time I saw my parents-in-law was at the wedding. Danielle and Jennifer, aged twelve and thirteen, recently took me aside to explain that they usually receive a Big Ticket Item for Christmas. A TV would be good. And I shouldn't expect them to go on any walks. Vacations are for resting.

"It's just a family Christmas," my husband says when I try to talk to him about it. "Everything will be fine." I don't remember him being so dim-witted.

I'm surprised to find myself wishing I could go home for Christmas to people who like to talk about food. It wasn't so bad sleeping with my nieces. It was sort of fun sneaking off with my cousin for another glass of wine and feeling superior to the mothers, our sisters, as they yelled at their kids. What was the problem with that? I'm having a hard time remembering.

On the Friday before Christmas I arrive home from work carrying bags of groceries to find everyone standing around the kitchen table. I hug my in-laws, kiss my husband, and try to listen to the children who are talking nonstop. Jennifer takes me aside to show me her new nose ring. She demonstrates that it is just a clip-on, and I try not to show relief. "But Dad won't let me wear it," she complains. "Tell him I can."

"Save it for when we go downtown later."

"He thinks he can tell me what to do. He is ruining my life." I look at this twelve-year-old with long blond hair, black jeans and T-shirt, and try not to laugh at her inflection. I remember my father making me wear little girl socks to church when I was her age, when the other girls were wearing stockings with garter belts. I wonder what she and my husband will talk about in thirty years. I can't imagine that it will be recipes.

The first, supposedly easy, meal has become a production. I try some new appetizers that set us behind in making the spaghetti. Fennel wrapped with prosciutto. Garbanzo beans dressed in oil and oregano. My husband, who claims his intake of garbanzo beans has increased geometrically since he met me, rolls his eyes. The slices of franchesi bread, salami, and mozzarella are eaten.

Usually I'm a good, if casual, cook, but tonight I can't seem to do anything right. I put too many red pepper flakes in the spaghetti sauce, and we have to dilute it with more tomatoes. This just causes it to be too hot and too tomatoey. The girls, who have been suspicious about the spaghetti from the start, want the sauce kept separate. By the time we eat, the noodles are a gelatinous ball. Only my husband believes that I never intended to include meatballs.

"This is like the time you forgot to put the egg in the hot and sour soup," Danielle says.

"This is just a tomato sauce. There weren't supposed to be meatballs."

"They're very easy to make, Karen. Maybe we can get the recipe from our mom." One meal down. Mixed reviews.

Saturday night I decide to try a new pork roast recipe. I had imagined the smell of pork and onions wafting through the house when my in-laws returned from mass. Unfortunately shopping took longer than I had expected, and the pork is still sitting in the butcher's paper when they walk through the door. My mother-in-law takes off her jacket and puts on an apron. I appreciate her help but feel guilty that she has to work so much.

We make slits in the pork and stuff garlic and olives in them. We peel beets and apples for a puree. We cut up parsnips, potatoes, carrots, and onions to bake. We're about an hour and a half late at this point, but things are coming together. I go look for my husband who is in the study working on his computer. Jennifer is there talking on the phone. "My mom," she mouths as I look at her. I know this is not true, but leave it. I lean over my husband and say, "Your dad is sitting by himself. Come out here and keep him company." He sighs, walks past his father to the kitchen, and asks if everyone is all right. He probably wants to make sure I'm not waving knives around at his family. I ask if he will hand me the cilantro and, after an initial search, he sits cross-legged in front of the open refrigerator, cleaning it out. With the refrigerator door open he has effectively trapped us all in the narrow kitchen. He is talking to his mother about the nuances of Macintosh hard drives while semiliquid plastic bags of vegetables and half-empty yogurt containers pile up on the floor around him. I assume he thinks he is contributing to the cooking effort, but I am not appreciative.

I take deep breaths. I baste the roast. I hug Danielle who has just mashed eggplant for a dip.

There is a scramble to light the candles, pour cola and pinot noir, and we sit down to dinner. They tell me the roast is good, but I can't tell. The kids won't even try a spoonful of the pink puree once they find out it is beets, but I knew that was a long shot. Jennifer, who has been beeped twice during dinner, excuses herself to go back to the phone. My husband takes me aside to say that it was delicious, but in the future it might be more efficient if I make only one dish and we get the rest takeout. I suggest it is his turn to do the dishes.

I guess the week is going well. Danielle and Jennifer are suspicious of any outdoor activity, thinking it might involve exercise, but they help with the cooking, suggest games of Scattergories, and are generally affectionate. My parents-in-law are easy to be with and appreciate the drive along the coast and other activities we've planned. My husband goes two days without turning on his computer. The problem is me. I keep making silly mistakes in the kitchen. I feel disconnected from my husband. I wish everyone would stay put, while I go downstairs and take a two-day nap.

It almost comes together on Christmas Eve. Danielle and Jennifer are enthusiastic about the presents from their grandparents, kiss their father when they open the ones from us, and make no mention of Big Ticket Items. I had decided to avoid a traditional dinner altogether, and in the afternoon we scrub mussels and clean shrimp for a seafood paella. My husband joins us again in the kitchen, this time sitting in front of the sink to straighten out the paper bags under the counter. I step over him and am hardly bothered at all. The paella is colorful in the middle of the table although Danielle, who has a future as a food critic, rightly points out that the mussels didn't all open and the rice was slightly undercooked. Jennifer stays at the table without making an excuse to get back to the phone. My father-in-law has three helpings of the jumbo shrimp, for which I am very grateful.

Everything is fine, but I feel something is missing. Even at midnight mass the priest seems determined to describe Mary as young and frightened, giving birth in a dirty cave alone without other women. I was expecting a miracle.

The next afternoon, when my husband came back from taking the girls home and his parents to the airport, he finds me reading in the living room. "Thank you," he says. "It was a wonderful Christmas."

"Did you think so?" I am bald-faced in my need for reassurance.

"It was better than wonderful. It was magic." It is my taciturn, practical husband that finds the right words. I listen very closely, knowing that he will not repeat them.

Waiting for the Pies

Davi Walders

for Marilyn, in memory

This is the moment before the year draws
its curtains and sleeps. Mums and garden
greens drowse above the platter's turkey
slivers, the last few cranberries.
The gravy bowl sits empty on spotted damask
among dolloped islands and crumbs.
Candles yawn, butter slips into silver
under dimmed lights. Dawn's chopping

blends into the past. The air hangs
thick as chestnuts in a room basted
with our gluttony. We eye each other
above stuffed stomachs and flushed
cheeks, waiting for the pies. Fat
with years, not wisdom, we will soon
stagger from dishes and detritus toward
the couch, chairs, the living room hearth.

He will again ask, "Why do we do this?"
and she, who now wears only elastic
waist bands to this yearly event, will respond
by unbuttoning one last button for old time's
sake. The debate will pit sweet potatoes
against mashed. Children grown, schooled,

returned, will ask again when we switched
from apple to pecan, why we still make pumpkin

when no one eats it. Conversation will focus
on who says "stuffing," who "dressing,"
who takes ice cream, who sticks to Cool Whip.
Ponderous issues will consume us until
we doze in front of sparking logs
before heading home. Suddenly, we fall silent.
For now, all we are required to do is to stare
at goblets, watching their reflected rainbows

and small tears form in the warm room.
Free to shift rituals, reduce consumption,
become reasonable and responsible,
we continue to resist, remain committed
to our recidivism. We float in cherished
time, waiting for the pies, thankful for
another year, the moment's sweet sameness,
the rich blessings of the day and each other.

In Fellini Time

Helen Friedland

As three generations
unfolded the length
of Thanksgivings
past, present,
and still to be,
dinner was metaphor
and magic.
Caught in Fellini time,
I was the baby
who cried,
the children
at table's end,
the young couples
in the middle,
and the soon to be
as old as I.
Amid the bounty of
sharing, love
and tender toasts,
I felt strangely whole,
all ages and ageless,
an ordinary woman
in an ordinary life,
content in knowing
that nothing could be
more extraordinary
than that.

Preparations for Seder

Michael S. Glaser

"Therefore, even if all of us were wise, all of us people of
understanding, all of us learned in Torah, it would still
be our obligation to tell the story of the exodus from Egypt,
for redemption is not yet complete."
—The Haggadah

Preparing schmaltz for matzo balls,
I peel the skin off chickens, scrape yellow fat
from pink meat, think of my father: how he stood
at the elbow of his mother, eating the "cracklings"
she'd hand down from the stove, morsels of meat
fried free of the fat, as she rendered schmaltz
years ago, in Boston.

Today, preparing for Seder, I think of Grandmother
as I salvage these tasty cracklings, relish them
for myself, hand them to my children as I cut more
and more fat from the chicken: how much harder
for her, hot before the wood stove, peeling bits
of fat from the muscle of chickens that ran
free in the yard.

Now the fat is plentiful, preserved with chemicals.
The echo of my father's voice calls out warnings
of carcinogens in the fat of animals and I wonder
what I am doing to myself, my children. But this

is the eve of Passover. I am making matzo balls.
My knife plunges under the skin for more fat.
I will not forsake the traditions of my ancestors.

At the Seder meal, we sip the chicken broth,
then cut into the matzo balls, savory
with marrow and garlic, parsley and schmaltz,
remembering forty years in the desert, the freedom
of the promised land, succulent and dangerous,
bobbing before us like these matzo balls we relish
and eat and praise the taste of, wanting more.

From the Kitchen of Barbara Kantro

MOM'S CHICKEN SOUP WITH MATZO BALLS

4- to 5-pound roasting chicken, quartered (heart, liver, and gizard removed)
4 to 5 celery stalks
2 to 3 large carrots, cut in half
1 large onion, cut in half
Few parsley sprigs
1/4 to 1/2 teaspoon white pepper
Salt to taste

Cover chicken with water and bring to a boil. Skim foam off top of water. Add onion, celery, carrots, parsley, and pepper. Simmer covered for approximately 1 1/2 hours. When chicken is falling off the bone, remove chicken, celery, and onions. Add salt to taste. Slice cooked carrots and return to soup. Cool soup. Soup will gel when it is cold. Skim majority of fat from top of soup. Serves 8 to 10.

EASY MATZO BALLS

Purchase Manischewitz Matzo Ball Mix and follow the recipe on the box. Add cooked matzo balls to warm soup. Makes about 10 matzo balls.

This Night, Different from All Others

Elaine Rothman

It wasn't until I was a grown woman that I learned that the Hebrew word "Seder" meant order. It gave me something to think about. I recalled all those childhood Passover Seders at my grandparents' house as spirited, noisy, chaotic, but not orderly. For one thing, Passover itself could arrive at any time in the spring, depending on the Jewish calendar, not on any specific date like New Year's Day or Columbus Day. Not even like Thanksgiving which always fell in November. Yet when I really thought about it, I realized there was a decided order to those long-ago Seders.

Everyone was expected at the Brooklyn brownstone where my father and his four brothers and four sisters had been born. Everyone meant Grandma and Grandpa's children, their spouses, and all the grandchildren, from tiny babies to teenagers. If a musician uncle had a gig on the West Coast, he rearranged his schedule to be home for Passover. If an aunt had a new baby a few days before the holiday, she could find plenty of places to rest at Grandma's and lots of people willing to help with the little one. So my mom, who worried that we'd get home too late for me to attend school the next day, did not have the option of staying home, even if she had wanted to.

The year I was seven, I was supposed to ask the Four Questions, an honor reserved for the youngest child who was old enough to put four sentences together. I had every word memorized and recited them in my head, lips moving, all the way over on the long trip from the Bronx. I couldn't permit Cousin Esther, who had asked them last year, to coach me if I hesitated.

When our family arrived, we were greeted with hugs and lavish kisses by what seemed like a hundred relatives. My little brother had the knack of squirming free and avoiding the inevitable cheek-pinching routine. Adults sat at the long dining room table, every extra leaf in place, while we children were relegated to the extension Grandpa put together for the occasion. Everyone who could read had a little Passover book on their dinner plate, provided free by the makers of Manischewitz wine.

At the proper moment in the Seder ritual, Grandpa peered over his eyeglasses and gave me the signal to contribute the part I had rehearsed. I was off and running, spilling "Wherefore is this night different from all other nights?" and all the rest of the questions, without pausing for breath, before the words could get stuck in my throat.

I saw all the proud adult faces beaming at me, as if from the wrong end of a telescope. I heard Cousin Esther mutter how "Mimi must have thought she had a train to catch." Meanwhile Grandpa was replying to my questions in Hebrew. I wouldn't have understood a word if I hadn't buried my face, red with relief and embarrassment, in the little book with the English translations on the left-hand page.

There was lots more Hebrew to be read, giving me the opportunity to run my finger along the English passages, as if I were truly following what was being said. My father's deep baritone rang out over all the other adult voices. His fluency was by far the best, and he didn't mind who knew it. Just like in the synagogue, Daddy would finish first and wait impatiently for the others to catch up.

At the children's table there was the usual chaos, except for Esther who sat like a bored princess. The family consisted mostly of boys, and my little brother was right at home with all of his male cousins. The boys made a great show of coughing and choking when the bitter herbs reached their end of the table. At the recitation of the ten plagues every boy dipped a finger into his wine glass, filled with water to which an eyedropper's worth of wine had been added, to see who could make the most purple spatters on Grandma's snowy tablecloth.

I didn't cough from the bitter herbs because I passed up the horseradish, knowing it would make my eyes water. I avoided the boiled potato and the parsley, because they had been dipped in salt water, and that was sure to make me gag. I did taste a spoonful of the chopped apple, walnut, and wine mixture on a tiny square of matzo. I had earned the reputation of being the only picky eater in the family and thought of myself as the "skinny *melink*" Cousin Esther once called me.

Neither Esther nor I engaged in the competition of stealing the matzo when Grandpa left his seat for the ritual of hand washing. We left that game to the boys. Grandpa, who needed that particular piece of unleavened bread before he could finish the readings, would pretend to be distraught at not finding it. The noisiest of the boys would produce it, from the place where he had hidden it, and every single one of the children would share in the reward. Last year Grandpa had given me a locket on a silver chain.

After the readings came the part I dreaded, the Seder meal. Over the racket of conversation, laughter, and even some arguments, Grandma, her daughters, and her daughters-in-law brought in an endless supply of bowls and platters filled with rich food. Also endless were the same old jokes. Aunt Gracie, the only unmarried daughter, had to take the hard-boiled egg with the scorched shell from the Seder plate, so she'd get herself a husband this year, God willing. And was Grandma serving goose, Uncle Max would ask? The one she had mistakenly plucked, thinking it had died from the cold, when it was only drunk on Grandpa's grape peelings?

There was no goose, only plate after plate of offerings like soup with golden globules floating on it, or veal cutlets in a thick brown gravy, or crisp potato kugel glistening with fat. I sat in dread of someone saying, "Try a little, Mimi. It'll put meat on your bones."

I would push a little food around on my plate, without tasting a morsel. As soon as I thought no one was watching, I would slip away from the table.

Recalling those old Seders, I am struck by the thought that my husband and I are the grandparents now, with all those other generations laid to rest. The Seder we make every Passover has kosher wine, Manischewitz booklets in Hebrew and English, and the kind of Seder plate Grandma used. Naturally there are far fewer faces around the table, but we sing the same songs after we have our modern fat-free, low-cholesterol dinner. The candles glow and the dishes shine, but somehow the Seder never has the order Grandma's did.

From the Kitchen of Barbara Kantro

POTATO KUGEL

2 pounds zucchini, grated

2 carrots, grated

1/2 large onion, grated

6-ounce package of Manischewitz Potato Pancake Mix

1 cup matzo meal

Scant 1 cup oil, any kind

12 egg whites, beaten almost stiff

Salt and pepper to taste

Add oil to zucchini and then mix other ingredients together. Pour into greased and heated 2-quart Pyrex dish. Bake at 350 degrees F for 45 minutes to 1 hour.

BARBARA'S BRISKET

1 cup catsup

1 cup water

2 tablespoons vinegar

1 tablespoon chopped onion

1 tablespoon prepared mustard

1/4 teaspoon pepper

4- to 5-pound beef brisket

Salt to taste (optional)

Combine all ingredients except brisket to create a marinade. Place meat in a shallow cooking dish. Pour marinade over meat. Cover and refrigerate overnight. Cover and bake at 325 degrees F for 3 to 3 1/2 hours (depending on size). Skim fat from sauce. Cool, slice, and serve with sauce.

Time, Place, and Uncle Dewey

Blanche Flanders Farley

My childhood home is a house in the country. It stands in the gently rolling fields of middle Georgia, on land that has been in our family for four generations. Jays and cardinals fly freely through the old orchard and into the giant pecan trees that shelter the yard. The wire fences sag. The dirt road washes out in rainy weather. But sunsets across those fields are second to none. It is never Christmas until I go there—where my parents still live, where my brother and I grew up, where my mother and her siblings grew up.

The look of this place has changed a bit since my grandfather's day. Lakeview, the ancestral home down the road, has been leveled. Only some of us remember it now, or recall our great-aunt Sudie who lived there last—how she planted the yard with sea oats and oleanders she dug up illegally in Savannah, how she walked up the road with a pistol in her apron in case of marauders.

Each of us has our own memories, our place in the time line. My granddaughter does not yet know that when she picks up pecans in my parents' yard she is gathering history. Someday, we will show her the postcard her great-great-grandmother wrote from this very place in 1929. She was urging a brother in Tennessee to take a share of the pecans she was sending back home by their sister. "Times are so hard," she wrote. "I hope to do better with gifts next year." By the next year, however, my thirty-eight-year-old grandmother had died of cancer, leaving her husband and seven young children behind. Today the trees stand tall, dropping their bounty from season to season.

Christmases have changed, too, from my childhood days. No more fireworks since the time a Roman candle backfired and burned my cousin Judy on the stomach. No more entire family gatherings, where cousins sleep on floor pallets and laughter drifts from the adults in the kitchen late on Christmas Eve. There are too many of us now. But some things do stay the same, or have, over time, become the norm. My daddy is still quick to whip out his pocket knife for anyone struggling with an overtaped gift. My daughter and niece, who love tradition, want us all to sit in the same chairs each year when we open presents. My brother always requests breakfast before the gifts. And my mother, who cooks enough food for a logrolling, still forgets at least one dish that she is heating in the oven. Every year, halfway through Christmas dinner, she suddenly stops eating and inquires, of all and sundry, "Where are my baby limas?"

Christmases past have already become the stuff of legend. We recall how my aunt Pat regaled us with stories of the elderly gentleman who sat beside her on the Greyhound bus from Florida one year. Hating bedpans, he had invented a potty chair that fit somehow under hospital beds—the beds capable of separating in the middle at the crucial moment. And there was the year in the 1940s when my uncles, in uniform, arrived late into the night—or, in some cases, did not arrive. Bing Crosby sadly sang "I'll be home for Christmas" on the scratchy phonograph. Even when we don't say so, we think longingly of the fires in all the fireplaces those years before gas heat—the crack of fat lighterd, the smell of oranges and evergreens, years when Santa brought simple non-electronic items like roller skates and cowboy suits. But there has always been a crèche on the table, a wreath on the door, a tree in the living room, the inevitable turkey and dressing in the oven.

In these shifting scenes, one of the most constant of constants is my mother's Uncle Dewey. At ninety-eight, he still lives alone and was recently driven into town to vote in the presidential election. He has been a part of every Christmas dinner I remember—coming in with a box of drugstore chocolates for my mother, his little hunting cap perched on his head. Until maybe ten years ago he walked up the steps unassisted, still wearing dentures. Now our cousin Stuart brings him over and helps him up the steps. He has home health care each day. But his memory is unfailing and, lack of teeth notwithstanding, he eats most anything and tries out every cake on the table. His highest praise has always been, "Now that is good cake. Yes sir, that is solid mahogany!"

As the bachelor uncle of the Lake clan, Uncle Dewey has long been the center of stories about the beautiful girl in Florida that he loved but felt he couldn't marry—she being something of a blue blood and he a humble farmer. These stories bring on speculation as to how lonely he is. Yet he has always seemed thoroughly contented, living in his not-so-insulated house, raising livestock, and farming. He refers to my mother and her sisters as "the girls" and assures my mother that she is not old yet.

A few years ago, Uncle Dewey decided to explain to my mother's family what had caused the long rift between their father and grandfather. This had long been a mystery. The two had lived only a few miles apart, but never spoke. "I thought it was time you chirren knew about that," Uncle Dewey said. (The chirren by then were into their sixties). The reason, as it turned out, was land. What else do Southerners feud over with such prolonged passion? His story alluded to some legal philanderings, shyster lawyers, and a lot of deception. Neither party was put in very good light.

"It wasn't right," Uncle Dewey said. "They ought to have made it up." A silence fell across the room then, everyone agreeing and looking out into space—perhaps recalling the day of their father's death, when their grandfather stood in tears in the hospital hallway, still refusing to enter the room. "Now that," my mother said, "is stubborn!"

The old man's kindly voice seemed to offer a closure of sorts—words from someone who had been there, someone who loved those stubborn men, in spite of themselves. Each year we marvel that he comes once again to the dinner. "Uncle Dewey's here," somebody announces. And we all bustle in from the kitchen and hall, to hug him and take his hat and catch up a little. He never forgets our names.

When he is no longer among us, I suspect we will all grow a little older. We will need him to be there, allowing the succeeding generations to go on being "chirren." We will need him to say, in tones that tell us life should be cherished, "Now that is good cake. That is solid mahogany!"

From the Kitchen of
Blanche Flanders Farley

FAMILY FRUIT SALAD

If you have apples left around the house after the holidays and if there's whipping cream left from garnishing the holiday pies, you are off to a good start on this fruit salad.

4 apples
3 bananas
1 small package of marshmallows
1/2 to 1 jar of maraschino cherries
1/2 pint of whipping cream

Whip cream and set aside. Peel, core, and cut apples into bite-sized pieces. Peel bananas, cut in half lengthwise, then cut crosswise into pieces. Put the cut fruit in a large glass bowl. Cut marshmallows small and add to mixture. Pour in whipped cream and mix with fruit and marshmallows.

(This could be dessert, but we just call it "salid.")

A Miner's Christmas

Cinda Thompson

When each of my grandfathers started work in the coal mines at the turn of the century, they made seventeen cents a ton. Maybe $1.75 a day during good times. Less during lean times. Farmers in the area could well make less until the harvest came in—if the harvest came in. Lean times included all times before the organization of an effective union, and any time a strike was called. Lean times surely included the Depression and the days of "modernization" as machinery replaced the strength of "manpower."

Christmas always meant that family of all ages—babies, teens, young singles and newly marrieds, grandmothers and grandfathers, uncles and twice-removed aunts, first and distant cousins, all who could make it, crowded into one house. No question there would be a dinner and a table set with a cloth.

Christmas also meant the coming of a stranger. If a fellow miner was out of work, if an old bachelor was caught sitting on the square with no place to go, one or the other of my grandfathers, at my grandmothers' own bidding, picked him up and brought him home. Anyone down on their luck was welcome, close kin and all. Christmas dinners could and would be made to stretch.

From the Kitchen of Cinda Thompson and Betty Thompson

CHICKEN AN' DUMPLIN'S

Chicken	Modern	Yesteryear
Meat	White or dark pieces as preferred. Best to buy boneless, or remove skin and debone after cooking in water.	Stewer will do. Check the coop.
Water	Add as needed.	Drawn and ready.
Salt/Pepper	Season to taste.	Store-bought.

Dumplings		
Flour (all purpose)	4 cups, plus extra to add as needed.	Bleached/sifted.
Eggs	2	Fresh. Check the henhouse.
Chicken broth	3 cans (6 cups total)	Chicken stock (5 to 6 cups).
Margarine	5 to 6 tablespoons	Churned butter.
Salt	1/2 teaspoon	Dash or so.
Water (boiling)	Add as needed.	

Serves 10 to 12. Add flour or water as needed for more. These dumplings are of a flatter variety, not the puffier type of more well-known recipes.

Chicken must be cooked beforehand. *Caution*: Use large pot. Do not cover. Salt if desired. Bring to a boil and simmer slowly, skimming off the fat as necessary. (This may be kept for stock, as can all "undesirable" parts of the chicken.) The stewing often takes at least 3 hours. The chicken can then be separated from skin and bone. Set aside in a covered dish to keep warm or store until time to make the dumplings. Should be warm or at room temperature before adding to dumplings.

Bring the broth and margarine to a boil. Beat the eggs separately, in a smaller bowl or cup. Put the 4 cups of flour in a large bowl, but have extra flour handy.

Add the eggs and about 2 cups of the hot broth to the flour. (Keep the rest of the broth hot and waiting. You may need to add water.) Add extra flour (or broth), as needed, to the mixture in the bowl until you can form a ball. If the dough is too sticky, more flour is needed. If it is too stiff, boiling broth or water should be added.

Roll out the mixture onto a floured surface (cutting board or foil) until thin, as thin as you can make it without tearing. Make sure your rolling pin and hands are also floured. You will probably not be able to roll all of the ball out at one time. Smaller balls can be worked with, but none of them (nor your hands or instruments) can be sticky.

Cut the flattened pieces with a sharp knife into strips approximately 1 1/2 inch wide (not more than twice a thumb's width) and 5 to 6 inches long. Drop them in the remaining boiling broth that was set aside.

Keep rolling and cutting until all the dumplings are in. Stir *lightly* with a fork. Boil about 15 minutes until done. Then stir in chicken last and simmer.

The recipe is trial-and-error but very adjustable. Richness of broth is judged by its yellow color. Add "yellow" (broth or stock—always boiling) instead of water if the number to be served increases by too many. More margarine may also be used instead. Again, more floured strips can be made up and added as the number of guests swells! Dumplings just have to be boiled first to get done. Chicken pieces can be added if cooked and handy, though a minimum amount is enough for tasty dumplings.

Mother's Three-Days-after-Christmas Dinner Menu

Cappy Love Hanson

Spam, either:
> baked,
> sautéed with onions, garlic, and oregano,
> in rice or noodle casserole,
> in grilled sandwiches with cheese, or
> scrambled with eggs.

Spam?

Yup. For years it appeared on our plates three days after Christmas. We had finished the turkey by then and were, Mother reasoned, jaded by all that rich holiday fare.

Besides, we had to either use up the Spam or throw it away. Mother hated to waste, though in this case the rest of us would have gladly let her make an exception.

How did we end up with cans and cans of Spam? During the Cuban missile crisis in the '60s, Mother stockpiled it, along with canned fruits and vegetables and gallon bottles of water, in the hall closet. We lived near Los Angeles and figured to be a high priority bombing target. If we weren't vaporized, we'd eat pretty well.

For years we teased Mother unmercifully about Spam, before finally admitting that planning for an emergency was a pretty good idea, and that she had our best interest at heart. Chance, after all, favors the prepared.

Of course, it was easier to forgive after we'd finally eaten it all.

From the Kitchen of Johny Van Dyke

CORN PUDDING

Recycle the leftover corn into a delicious soufflé side dish.

3 eggs
2 cups whole kernel corn
2 cups milk
1/3 cup finely chopped onion
1 tablespoon butter
1 teaspoon sugar
1 teaspoon salt (optional)

Beat eggs lightly; add corn, milk, onion, butter, sugar, and salt. Pour into a 1 1/2 quart baking dish and bake for 40 minutes at 350 degrees F. Let stand for 10 minutes before serving.

If Diamonds Grew on Orange Trees

Pamela Ditchoff

Alongside cousin Marilyn's lattice-topped mincemeat pie, my sister's spectacular chocolate Yule log, and my platter of Christmas cookies sugared and spangled like jewels, Mother's orange cake looks homely. The frosting on the two round layers is so pale, it's barely orange, except for bits of bright rind here and there. However, tonight, as with every Christmas night in my memory, when relatives and friends pull on their coats and boots, gather their presents, and wrap leftover turkey, deviled eggs, scalloped corn, candied yams, cranberry bread, and cookies, not a single slice of orange cake will remain for the taking.

Mom's is a delicious, mouth-delighting cake, as substantial and old-fashioned as my mother. Part of the cake's appeal is the fact that she bakes it only once a year on Christmas Eve. No matter how I begged her to make one for my birthday when I was young, she wouldn't budge. Even when I whined that plaintive plea of children, "Why not?" she would answer emphatically, "If diamonds grew on orange trees, they'd lose their sparkle."

As soon as I was grown and living on my own, I baked that orange cake in the middle of September. While mixing the ingredients, I couldn't help thinking of Mom's kitchen: the old Mixmaster and its three white nesting bowls; her long-handled wooden spoons; the burst of citrus as she sliced the oranges and let me twist each half over the juicer; the tree lit and tinseled in the living room; Bing Crosby carols playing on the radio; Dad popping his head in the kitchen, sniffing with a Cheshire cat grin. My orange cake tasted great, but baking it had the forced quality of a Christmas in July sale. I thought I finally understood the meaning of Mom's mysterious maxim. But I didn't fully understand until this Christmas day.

Aunt Emily, at seventy-six, is five years older than my mother. She and her husband were unable to have children, and since his death three years ago, Aunt Emily increasingly wanders in time. She'll be talking about yesterday's *Oprah* show and with the next breath recall a train trip to Chicago in 1950.

At the moment, she's lifting a forkful of orange cake to her mouth. Everyone else finished their meal twenty minutes ago, and Mom and Dad are sitting on the couch with my niece between them. Aunt Emily pokes me with her sharp little elbow and points her fork at my parents. "Remember the first time she made this cake? She was so embarrassed I had to drag her to the party. That's the night she met Ronnie. Christmas Eve of '42, wasn't it?" Aunt Emily asks, her whole face drawn into a question mark.

"I don't know, Aunt Em," I answer, and she smiles and pats my hand indulgently.

"It was '42; Sissy's third year of high school. I was engaged to Bill and working at the Nash Calvinator plant; didn't have time to make a dish for the party, and Mother, bless her heart, she could bang that tambourine to beat the band, but she couldn't cook. Around Christmastime, they'd stand on the corner of Washington and Michigan Avenue in their uniforms, Dad playing the trumpet, Harry Foster pounding the bass drum. Sometimes, Sissy rang the bell over the kettle. Cold, let me tell you. Mother's cheeks would be as red as her hair under that bonnet. *Serve others*; that's the Salvation Army's motto!" Aunt Emily jerks her chin, looks at me as if I'm supposed to answer.

"You said Mom was embarrassed the night of the party?" I pry, eager to unlock the mystery of the orange cake.

"What party?" Aunt Emily blinks twice. "I was wandering; where was I?"

I slip my arm around her waist. "I love your stories, Aunt Em. The church party in '42?"

"Yes, members were asked to bring a dish, so Sissy used a recipe she'd clipped from the newspaper. Lucky Mother couldn't bake or she wouldn't have had the ingredients. What with rationing, sugar was hard to keep, and oranges were rare as hen's teeth for folks poor as we were." Aunt Emily takes a bite of cake and licks her lips as if remembering a time when sweets were few and far between.

"The Sunday before Christmas, Dad brought home two oranges they'd given him at the Army. Mother didn't care for the fruit, so she packed them in Sissy's school lunch bag. But Sissy took them out and hid them in her room because WELFARE was stamped on those oranges in big blue letters." Aunt Emily leans close and whispers, "Didn't want the kids at school to see them. You know how kids are."

I do know how kids are; at the moment I feel like a child who has snooped in a secret drawer while her parents are away.

"Well, when she made the cake for the church party, squeezed the oranges to get the juice out, the ink came off and stained her hands with blue splotches. We tried scrubbing—that lye soap Mother had could take the hide off a mule, but not welfare ink off Sissy's hands."

Mom's hands are now tying a Christmas ribbon in her great-granddaughter's hair. She's always been proud of her hands, which have remained youthful, plump and white as doves. My throat tightens and my cheeks flush; she wouldn't want me imagining those lovely hands stained with her private shame.

"Like I said, I had to drag her along the street down to the church. She made me carry the cake in and put it on the table, and then she hid her hands all evening by crossing her arms or sitting on them. Harry Foster brought Ronnie along as a guest; they were both students at MSC then. Ronnie ate two pieces of Sissy's cake, and he said to Frankie, 'I'm going to marry the girl that baked this cake.' And he did!" Aunt Emily hoots and winks at me. "One year later, on Christmas Eve, he gave her a diamond engagement ring, sneaked it into her piece of orange cake while she was getting coffee." Aunt Em finishes the last bite of cake and licks her fork. "Good as this cake is, it's a shame Sissy only bakes it once a year."

"If diamonds grew on orange trees, they'd lose their sparkle," I murmur, more with reverence than with mystery.

From the Kitchen of Pamela Ditchoff

MOTHER'S ORANGE CAKE

3/4 cup shortening

1 1/2 cups sugar

3 eggs

4 teaspoons baking powder

1/2 cup orange juice

Orange rind, grated

1 tablespoon lemon juice

3 cups flour

1/2 cup water

Frosting

2 cups powdered sugar

1/4 cup butter, softened

3 tablespoons orange juice

1 squirt lemon juice

1/2 teaspoon grated lemon rind

Cream shortening; add sugar and mix until light. Add eggs, one at a time, beating after each. Add rind. In another bowl, sift dry ingredients three times. Add dry ingredients alternately with liquids to creamed mixture. Pour into two 8-inch round, greased, and floured cake pans. Bake for 30 minutes at 350 degrees F. Turn out on wire racks to cool. Frost.

The Ceramic Camel

Eileen Murphy

Whenever somebody knocks too hard on the front door of our house, the little figurines in the nativity set that we set on the hall table every Christmas jump. And absolutely every Christmas, when Aunt Claire bangs on the door, the third Wise Man who stands closest to the edge of the table next to his ceramic camel falls on the floor. It's happened every year for as long as I can remember, and this year I decided to be prepared. Aunt Claire's ETA was 3:00 on Christmas Eve afternoon, so I stationed myself next to the manger set at about 2:30. (Aunt Claire is perpetually early.) Not two minutes after I took up my post, I heard footsteps on the front walk. Quickly, I cupped my hand around the third Wise Man and his camel. The rest of the statuettes danced as Aunt Claire pounded on the door, but the damage wasn't too severe, although St. Joseph teetered for a few seconds after the earthquake arrested.

"Can you get the door, Timmy?" Mom called to my little brother.

"Mandy's closer!" the tinny little voice replied.

I heard my mother sigh. "Mandy . . . ," she began plaintively.

I groaned. "But Mom . . . ."

The banging resumed.

"*Will somebody answer the door!*" bellowed my older brother Dave.

"Mandy's getting it!" Timmy sang.

"I am not!"

"Yes you are!"

"No I'm not!"

My mother brushed by me then, and put her hand on the doorknob. "Jack, Claire's here!" she called to my father, her voice strained with false cheerfulness.

Dad appeared, a much-practiced expression of joy plastered on his face. "Smile," he prompted me as he passed. I reluctantly forced the corners of my mouth up.

We all feel the same way about Aunt Claire. She's much older than Dad, her brother, and everything about her is long and skinny, especially her teeth and fingers. She pencils her nonexistent eyebrows in every morning, giving her face a constant look of surprise. Her thin lips look as if she's just been sucking a lemon, and she wears old-lady perfume. Worst of all, she calls me Amanda.

"What took you so long?" was the first thing she said to us. Claire had only one small bag with her, which she promptly handed over to my father to be taken to the guest room. Her eyes passed over us and the front hall, taking on an expression that had my mother cleaning weeks before Claire's arrival in an effort to avoid it.

"You look wonderful, Claire," Mom attempted fruitlessly.

Aunt Claire pursed her lips at my mother disapprovingly. "Vitamins, Janet, work wonders. You should take some." Her frown deepened. "And where are the boys? They don't even get up to greet company? Some gentlemen they turned out to be."

Gentlemen? Timmy and Dave? What century was she living in, anyway?

Then she turned to me. I steeled my nerves.

Aunt Claire clucked her tongue. "Amanda, what did you do to your hair?" she said disapprovingly.

My hand instinctively flew to my hair, tucking behind my ear a lock that had fallen loose from my hasty ponytail. "I . . . uh, nothing."

She shook her head. "That must be it." She stroked her own greying tresses, arranged perfectly as usual. I bit back my reply. Dave, who had finally heaved himself off the couch long enough to say hello, shot me a sympathetic look.

I made my escape while Aunt Claire gave Dave the once-over. I found Timmy in the living room with Strawberry, the family dog.

"Thanks for getting the door before," I said, raising an eyebrow. I couldn't really scold him, though; who could blame him?

"I'm hiding," he informed me.

I shook my head. "Best to go now. It's worse if she has to look for you." Timmy was still too young to really understand that stuff; all he knew was that he didn't like Aunt Claire.

So he just sat there. I pitied him. He really didn't know what he was in for. Sure enough, I heard Aunt Claire call out, "Timothy! Where are you?" Only then did Timmy drag himself to his feet and head for the hallway. I gestured a blessing toward him, as if he was going off to battle. "Watch the manger," I added. "She's dangerous."

We all struggled through Christmas Eve dinner, for Aunt Claire's sake. There was none of the usual banter across the table, or lively arguments. In fact, there was very little conversation at all; "Pass the salt" invoked a lecture about sodium intake, and Timmy's excusing himself hastily to go to the bathroom spawned another lecture about manners, not to mention bladder control. I wanted to tell her that he only had to go because she made him so nervous, but just when I opened my mouth Dave kicked me in the shin. It hurt, and I opened my mouth to yelp, so he stuffed a roll in my mouth. It tasted good. I shut up.

"You're lucky I did that," Dave said to me later in the living room, when Aunt Claire had excused herself to go "freshen up."

I rolled my eyes. "You shoulda let me tell her off. She deserved it."

Dad patted my shoulder sympathetically. "I know how you feel, Sport, but she means well. She's just a little hard to stomach sometimes."

"Like that quarter I swallowed when I was five," Dave put in, ever helpful.

"I don't like her," Timmy announced. He was lying on the floor with his head under the tree. He did that every year.

"Hot chocolate, anyone?" Mom offered, coming in with a tray. She set it next to the boxes of ornaments on the coffee table. It was a Christmas Eve tradition to trim the tree as a family. I was eager to get started without Aunt Claire. Dad and Dave started untangling the lengths of colored lights and replacing dead bulbs. Mom unearthed boxes of tinsel, while Timmy started searching for the green reindeer. (We have these ornaments in the shape of painted wooden reindeer, and Blitzen is green. No one can explain it.) I hunted for the little sailor that we got in Myrtle Beach a few summers ago. We were working blissfully when Mom commented, "I can't figure out where all those ornaments you kids made in kindergarten with your pictures in them are."

Dave and I exchanged a conspiratorial look. "Don't know, Mom," Dave said smoothly. Truth was, we had hidden those stupid ornaments years ago.

"Amanda, would you come here for a moment?" Aunt Claire called from the guest room.

Darn it. I'd almost forgotten she was still here.

Dad saw my hesitation. "Go on, Sport," he prompted.

"Been nice knowing you," Dave added. "I'll be glad to open your presents for you tomorrow, since you'll be in the morgue and all."

I smiled smugly at him. "Go right ahead. She gave me a Barbie doll last year anyway."

Dave scowled at me, but that didn't stop him from humming the Death March as I trudged up the stairs.

Aunt Claire was standing over her suitcase. She knew without turning around that I was at the door. "Come in, Amanda," she invited. I stepped in nervously.

When she turned to face me, she was holding something in her hand. "Your Christmas present," she explained, her voice softer than usual. "I know I should wait until tomorrow, but it'll be so crazy, with your cousins coming and all, that I thought I'd give it to you now."

What is it this year, Barbie shoes? I wondered silently. I prepared myself to look thrilled with whatever it was, but when I saw it, I was genuinely pleased. "A locket," I said softly.

"It was your grandmother's," Aunt Claire told me. "She got it when she turned sixteen, and since you'll be turning sixteen this year . . . " She smiled at me. "I thought it would be appropriate."

I was speechless. I don't usually go in for jewelry and stuff, but the locket was really beautiful. And my grandmother died before I was born. I got a lump in my throat.

"Open it up," Aunt Claire urged.

I slipped my fingernail between the two sides of the necklace and pried it open. Inside was a picture. "Of me?"

She smiled again. "No, dear. That's me when I was your age. I was a lot like you, you know. Speaking before I thought." But she wasn't reprimanding; she sounded almost amused.

I absorbed this. Did it mean that I would end up like Aunt Claire when I grew up?

An hour ago that would've seemed like a fate worse than death. But now . . . now that didn't sound so bad at all.

When some people talk about their family tree,
they trim off a branch here and there.

—E.C. McKenzie

Secret Ingredient

Mary Eileen Price

In every family there has to be at least one member who thinks of himself/herself as a top-notch cook. They usually have one good recipe and serve this same dish every time you eat with them. Our master chef was my Uncle Albert. He was the kindest, sweetest, gentlest man anyone would want to know, and we loved him dearly. Wherever we lived, holidays meant Uncle Albert and his black leather shopping bag, filled with provisions for his specialty. He would go through the ritual of chasing us all out of the kitchen, demanding total privacy when he cooked. It was a planned meal every time, usually the night before the big day. We all knew he was making pot spaghetti. He always did. It got the name from the way he served it. He didn't believe in frills and set the pot right on the table. He was always mysterious about this recipe, insisting on preparing it alone.

One Christmas Eve in Toledo, Mama got pretty testy and sneered, "For heaven's sake, Albert, you don't have to be overprotective. We all know your secret ingredient! It's," she paused, then shouted, "*sugar!*"

We all gasped. Uncle Albert turned white, standing perfectly still for a moment, his back toward Mama. He slowly turned to face her, and with a smirk, asked, "Brown . . . or white?"

From the Kitchen of Mary Eileen Price

UNCLE ALBERT'S POT SPAGHETTI

1 pound thin spaghetti
1 quart tomato juice
1 can tomato paste
1 pound ground chuck
1 onion, chopped fine
1/4 cup brown sugar
Pinch of salt
1 tablespoon margarine or butter

Bring three quarts of water to a boil in a large pot; add the salt and margarine or butter. Break the spaghetti in half and add it to the boiling water; cook until tender. While the spaghetti is cooking, sauté ground beef with the onion until cooked, but not hard. Drain the cooked spaghetti. Mix the tomato paste with the juice and add to the pot. Stir in the meat. Sprinkle the brown sugar over the spaghetti and fold it in. Cook 5 to 10 minutes to blend flavors. Serve with garlic bread, made by buttering each slice of bread, sprinkling with garlic powder, and browning in the oven.

The Holiday Maneuver

Linda Ann Ford

My childhood memories of holidays always revolved around my mom cooking the five-course, midday meals. When I think about those times—the wonderful foods, the kitchen smells—it always brings a smile to my face.

My dad always made the salad for our meals. He made the best Lebanese salad with Greek olives, feta cheese, herbs, and spices. The dressing was his own making, something he learned from his mother, and as the years went by, he continually improved on it. He always used iceberg lettuce, which he chopped by hand and added to the salad with the greatest of care.

One holiday everyone had come down—aunts, uncles, sisters, nieces, and of course, all the in-laws. Halfway into the salad course, I noticed that my sister was turning red and starting to cough. Then her coughing stopped, and she was holding her throat as though trying to gasp for air. The whole family watched in horror. Finally, after what seemed forever, she somehow managed to dislodge the piece of lettuce that had gotten stuck in her throat. Having composed herself, she proceeded on to the next course, skipping the rest of her salad.

After everyone had gone home, my mom and I were cleaning up and putting away the leftovers. Dad was sitting at the table reading his daily newspaper. While drying the last of the dishes, Mom said, "I'm really glad your sister got that piece of lettuce up. I was so afraid I would have to do the Hick-Hick Maneuver, and I never did learn how to do it properly." My dad raised his head, looked at her, and said, "Betty, it's not the *Hick-Hick*. It's the *Hemlock* Maneuver!" I didn't say a word, but it took all I had to keep a straight face. I'm sure Dr. Heimlich would have appreciated the moment.

God could not be everywhere and therefore he made mothers.

—Jewish Proverb

Looking Back

Janice J. Heiss

Whenever I visit my home in the Midwest, I thumb through my parents' old photo albums. I still shake my head at the innumerable, identical photos Dad places side-by-side in the albums.

So that all adults would appear in each shot, we painstakingly rotated photographers round-robin style. In addition, we routinely took the same shot several times to get it right. A lot could go wrong during these photo sessions. A child might close his or her eyes during the camera flash, sneak away to watch TV or go to the bathroom, or some insensitive soul might not include the dog(s) in the picture.

As official photographer, my father prolonged the agony. He bought every gadget that came to market, but he never knew how to operate his state-of-the-art equipment. It seemed to take him hours to read the instructions, which he read like a Dostoyevsky novel. Despite this, one Thanksgiving my father took over fifty shots with his supposedly self-loading camera that turned out to be filmless.

"Thanksgiving, 1956," appears under one representative picture. I remember this shot. Grandma Iris, wearing her signature apron of blue and yellow irises, poses center stage. In the photo, everyone has a "say cheese" smile. All the men are looking one way out of the corner of their eyes—toward the TV. Cousin Lisa and the crybaby are crying. Their parents simultaneously smile for the camera while they, under their breath, threaten to give the little brats a spanking as soon as they can get their hands on them. This makes the little brats wail louder. Grandpa Harry, the unwilling patriarch, always responding with "Aw, shit!" when roused from his Queen Anne armchair in a dark corner of the living room, gazes into the camera with ennui and stands apart, as if he doesn't want to be contaminated.

So there we all stand, a flashing moment in the world, at Dempster and Grosse Point Road in Skokie, Illinois, three blocks from the Maple Tree Village Shopping Center. I love many of these people, almost against my will. Over the years, they haven't changed much; all that has really changed is what they own. The more I gaze at this photograph, the more I realize how shopping connected us, how products were the bedrock of our community, how our love of Wilson tennis balls, Tupperware, and Fords was our common language. If we dressed the same, we were the same. Nothing more needed to be said or done to establish our bond.

I see the tenets of our faith. Buying was inherently good; it was a duty to God and to country. Consuming gave you an identity while it helped others: the sales people, the stores, the manufacturers, the farmers, the entire economy, and the nation. After all, to use a common Lerner expression, "Everyone has to eat." Doing business was the primary way to cultivate relationships with people throughout one's life.

I still have fond memories of Mom and me on Saturdays in the sanctuary of Hillcrest Shopping Mall. Memories of big sales. Of the charge we got grabbing sales items off racks, pushing our way through clothes and other shoppers in the free-for-alls. There's nothing like it! We couldn't get enough.

I have regrets. Watching Aunt Daisy consumed by consumerism, nothing left of her but charge cards. (The family recently finished paying off all her charges.) Still, whenever anyone argued with my aunts that shopping, that materialism, had no meaning, they laughed and answered: "Life has no meaning, so why should shopping?"

I survived my childhood growing up shopping in the suburbs. And, as much as I might criticize my family for their materialism, I get some comfort from all my things. Somehow, what kills us, keeps us alive.

The Singing Men of Cleveland

Linda Nemec Foster

All my childhood memories of Christmas revolve around visiting family and friends in Cleveland, Ohio, where I was born and raised and where most of my extended family still lives. Every Christmas Eve, my father, mother, younger sister, and I would visit my mother's side of the family (which included lots of uncles, aunts, and cousins) to have a huge, festive meal. Since we were second-generation Polish immigrants, this night of *Wigilia* was filled with traditions from the old country such as the sharing of *oplatek*, unblessed communion bread, as well as those from the new country like singing about Rudolph the Red-Nosed Reindeer.

On Christmas morning, we would go to church then unwrap our presents. Imagine the patience that took for a child! In the afternoon we would visit my father's side of the family and have another huge meal of kielbasa, turkey, ham, potatoes, vegetables, my grandmother's incomparable dressing, and a ton of pastries.

The most memorable event of the day (besides opening our gifts) occurred in the early evening. The women would be in the kitchen—doing the dishes, putting the food away—and the adult men would all gather around to sing *koleda*, Polish Christmas carols. My father, grandfather, and uncles would sing away—each with a big cigar in one hand and a beer in the other. For some reason (which was never clear to me), only the men sang—never the women. It was always off-key, it was never melodic, but in my memory it remains some of the most beautiful music I've ever heard.

From the Kitchen of Linda Nemec Foster

MY MOTHER'S "EAT IT OR ELSE" TURKEY HASH

2 cups of finely cut turkey leftovers
1 (8-ounce) can of sliced white potatoes, drained
1 (8-ounce) can of green beans (preferably French cut)
1 cup of leftover turkey dressing (optional)
Dash of salt
Dash of pepper

In a large skillet, slowly brown the finely cut turkey pieces for about 10 minutes. Gradually add the potatoes, green beans, and (if desired) dressing. Stir well. Add salt and pepper. Stir again. Cover and cook the entire mixture on low for about 20 to 30 minutes. "Now eat it," as my mother would say.

Serves 4 to 6 (depending on your enthusiasm for leftovers).

Memories to Warm the Season

Julia Taylor Ebel

Each year the box of ornaments is carried up from the basement. Each year the same ornaments are hung on the tree. This part of Christmas I can count on.

Every ornament is dear to me. The felt birds I made for my mother twenty-four years ago are there. In her absence, they have returned to me and now hang among ornaments she made for us. A branch holds one marked, "John's 1st Christmas, 1976," a gift from his aunt. Yarn Santas made over milk jug rings, products of elementary classrooms, have places of honor. Curled paper ornaments my sons proudly made in secret some years ago adorn branches. So do the painted and decoupaged ones my son and I made together when he was five and recuperating from a tonsillectomy in early December. Those received as gifts from friends, now miles away, and remembrances from students—they are all there too, and each one holds a memory.

Like the blocks of an old quilt made from scraps of this and bits of that, ornaments on my tree have histories in many colors and hues. Our tree is a patchwork of our lives, a reminder of our family story: our growing together, our expansion, our celebrations, our losses, our adjustments, and our expected but still painful separations. Mothers know those feelings.

The tree itself is a mirror of all the Christmas trees I searched the woods to find with my family, then cut and carried home. As a child my father carried the tree. Later my husband and still later sons assumed that role. Even the skirt beneath the tree wraps memories, for I made it the first year my husband and I were together.

I occasionally walk through Christmas shops with exquisitely decorated trees and manufactured ornaments, yet I find nothing there for me. Instead, such perfect trees seem a bit empty and sad. Where are the memories? Where are the people who are a part of those trees?

Over the years, my family, like all families, has known change. We have known the idealistic joy of youth, and we have known pride as we watched our sons grow in right ways. As I look at the ceramic ornaments lovingly crafted by my mother especially for me, I remember the unconditional love of both my parents, and painfully I remember their sacrifice to cancer and heart failure. I remember the emptiness of their absence. The patchwork of our tree holds reminders of change.

Atop our tree now shines a star. Using scraps saved from the wedding dress my mother sewed for me, I made it last year as a gift for my family. Now, after twenty-five years, someone in my family is tall enough to reach the treetop and tie the star on. That person is my son.

With sons in college, with age tiptoeing across our lives, I can expect no more constancy at Christmas than at other times. Life is change. Good memories, though, offer us strength and encouragement. Memories will remain and continue to warm the Christmases of the future as they do today. I shall hang mine on our tree.

No Gravy, No Hash

Sara E. Sanderson

Our whale of a frozen turkey bobbed up and down at the far end of the bathtub, away from the warm rushing current intended to speed up thawing. Home was new that year, and we meant to have every holiday tradition—from lavish feast to Granddad McCune's favorite turkey hash the day after.

One problem though was as newlyweds we hadn't thought to buy a turkey ahead of time. Walking home late Christmas Eve from our hospital research jobs, we assumed the corner store would have one; it did. One. And it weighed in at over twenty-five pounds.

Ron carried it; we'd stop. My arms could barely circle the beast, but I offered to help. I got about one block before I was sure it gained weight; I had to pass it back again. Eventually we got it home and upstairs to our tiny apartment.

I dialed Mom; she would know what to do. "How long does it take a turkey to defrost?" I hoped for an easy answer. I could hear my sister, Barb, in the background, playing carols on the piano. Pangs of "I want my Mommy" grabbed me by the throat. This was the first year going home for Christmas was just a few blocks journey. At that moment I longed for snowbound Buffalo, Dad decorating the tree with crinkly tin icicles carefully saved from last year, and Mom making rum hard sauce for the plum pudding. I could almost see the roaring fire and smell the pine boughs arranged in the heirloom Madonna vase.

"Why Sara, you can't get it done in one night," answered Mom. "Can she, George?" she wavered. We tossed ideas across the miles, decided hot water in the bathtub was worth a try. What the heck. Ron threw it in the tub, drew a hot stream, and we waited.

I had plenty to do: chop celery and onion, tear up bread for stuffing. Another phone call: "Mom, I can't find those little round molds you gave me. What can I use for the tomato aspic?" No, I wasn't sure Ron would like it, but we always had rounds of tomato aspic on leaf lettuce with a dab of mayonnaise. And I was determined to bring "home" to our little apartment.

Time marches on and so does thawing. By a fashionably late hour the next day, we celebrated our first Christmas dinner in our new home. I guess it was delicious; I can't remember. All I remember is pride, love, and knowing there'd be lots of leftovers. Tomorrow I'd treat my new husband to another family tradition—the much praised hash.

I cleaned up, carefully picking every morsel of meat off that huge carcass, putting the broth in a tall container to let the fat rise. I tried to remember how my mother did everything, tried to do the same.

The day after Christmas, Ron pampered me with breakfast in bed. And he cleaned up! That floored me; my father always retreated to doze behind a newspaper. What had times come to when men helped in the kitchen!

Afternoon rolled around, dusk settled in; it was time to make turkey hash. Taking the white turkey meat from the refrigerator I began to search for my huge jar of broth.

"Ron," I called. "When you made breakfast, did you do something with my jar of broth?"

"You mean that tall thing of grease? I used it for the bacon fat, and then it was full, so I threw the whole thing out. Why?"

I wailed and ranted—tears weren't enough. My soul split. Visions of being the home-maker vanished; home was supposed to have hash.

We survived. And we had a wonderful winter that year; lots of long walks, making snowmen, sharing hot cocoa. And a freezer full of turkey, for sandwiches. No gravy, no hash, just sandwiches. I didn't know then you could buy broth in a can, and I certainly wasn't going to ask my mother.

From the Kitchen of Lori Van Dyke

PERSIMMON PUDDING

2 ripe persimmons
3 eggs
1 1/4 cup light brown sugar
1 cup flour
1 teaspoon baking powder
1 teaspoon baking soda
1/2 teaspoon salt
1/2 cup melted butter
1 1/2 cups light cream
2 teaspoons cinnamon
1 teaspoon ginger
1/2 teaspoon freshly grated nutmeg
1 cup chopped dates
1/2 cup chopped walnuts

Preheat oven to 325 degrees F. Press persimmons through a sieve to create 2 cups persimmon pulp. Use traditional persimmons (not the Japanese variety).

Beat in remaining ingredients. Bake in a greased 9 x 9-inch baking pan for 1 hour. Serve at room temperature with cream sauce. Recipe follows.

CREAM SAUCE

2 cups milk
4 egg yolks, slightly beaten
1/4 cup sugar
1 teaspoon salt
1 teaspoon vanilla
2 tablespoons brandy

Scald milk in double boiler; add egg yolks, sugar, and salt. Continue cooking in double boiler, stirring constantly until the sauce thickens. Remove from heat and stir occasionally as the sauce cools to release steam. Just before serving, stir in vanilla and brandy.

Polishing the Silverware

Bernice Rendrick

By increments, impatience leads
away, suggests I skip extra
spoons and forks, pare back.

Stubborn, I said no tree this year.
The younger generation coaxes, so
a bough sparkles with white lights.

As a child this was my job
to improve the tarnished ground.
Raise flowers from soot.

Scrolls gleam, tines are lined
up like toy soldiers, scrutinized.
Get the bird out. Defrost!

Now do the Finnish coffee spoons
and forks, their course altered
to pickles and cranberry relish.

Write one last Christmas card.
Excuse to walk to the mailbox
past trees aromatic with pine.

I'm not ready yet! Bread puffed
as if to explode, still to braid.
Linen tablecloth to iron.

I'm growing tired. Daughter calls
from work, no time, says systematize,
prioritize. Our rituals are dying,

I must accept change and simplify.
But the spoons shine like winter
moons, we'll be together.

Let the star burn with love.

Finding Christmas

Jean Blackmon

What I wanted was a cozy family Christmas. I wanted the scent of gingerbread, a real tree hung with strings of popcorn and cranberries, and four children tearing open gifts on Christmas morning. Instead, I have plaster dust, gift certificates under a plastic tree, and four cranky teenagers who will do well, even on Christmas day, to drag themselves out of bed before noon.

It's Christmas Eve. I'm baking thumbprint cookies in a portable roaster in my bedroom. I'm also folding laundry. On my bed lies a mountain of clean underwear. Half of it belongs to people whom, a year ago, I did not know. A cookie sheet with little balls of dough sits on top of my dresser. Into each dough ball I press my thumbprint. Carefully. This is the only Christmas baking I will do. I set the cookies in the roaster, replace the lid, and set the timer.

The roaster belongs to my new husband, Paul. I'm giving it a trial run before I trust it with our twenty-two-pound Christmas turkey.

Last January I met Paul at a camera show in Old Town. I was selling my gear to pay bills. He bought my Nikon F3 and three lenses plus filters all neatly packed in a Haliburton case. As I took his money and handed him the gear, a fist knotted in my stomach. He said, "Don't worry. Your camera will have a happy home. Can I buy you dinner?"

We ate wrapped tortilla sandwiches at a little place next door. By September we had decided to marry.

We took his two daughters and my two sons, all products of ill-fated first marriages, to brunch and told them we would marry in two weeks. Their silence seemed eternal. They looked at us as if we'd just announced a trip to Jupiter. Then my son Brad said, "Cool, Mom. Now you can get your camera back."

Paul and I married in Old Town, in a little chapel courtyard overgrown with trumpet vines, three blocks from where we met. Our parents came, along with a few friends, and, of course, our children—his Betsy, fifteen, and Anna, thirteen; my Carter, sixteen, and Brad, fourteen.

The kids rolled their eyes and snickered every time Paul and I got near each other.

After a one-night Hilton honeymoon, we moved everyone into my house because it was larger than Paul's apartment. My two boys are in one bedroom, his two girls in another, and Paul and I are in the third. We hired the only builder in town who would promise to enlarge the rest of the house before Christmas.

The tearing out phase progressed on schedule. The rebuilding phase did not. First, a snowstorm made it impossible to finish the roof. Then an eighteen wheeler speeding through the canyon rear-ended the delivery truck that carried our new windows, and they had to be reordered. A glitch in the new oven forced us to send it back to the factory. The refrigerator we picked was no longer available. And last week the carpenters took off for the holidays.

Three months ago, on our wedding day, when Paul, clean shaven and smelling of citrus, bent to kiss me, I believed our marriage was well considered. I had not, however, considered the possibility of cooking Christmas dinner in a portable roaster in the bedroom. And I had not considered myself an incompetent mother. But I am. Right now I don't know where any of the children are, except maybe Carter. I would guess he's parked somewhere making out with his girlfriend, and there's nothing I can do about it.

The front door opens.

"Who's there?" I call.

No answer. I make my way down the minefield that is our hallway, stepping over paint cans, hammers, scraps of drywall. I fumble to open the plastic curtain that separates the heated part of our house from the cold and step into our soon-to-be living room. It's Anna, carrying gifts wrapped in foil paper with large bows. She looks at me with sullen eyes through long straight bangs and says, "Hi."

Paul follows, carrying more gifts. "Smells like Christmas," he says.

"Cookies," I say. "I'm testing the roaster."

He places the gifts on the concrete floor near the little plastic tree and looks at me. "You look tired."

Anna drops her gifts beside his. "This is not Christmas," she says. "This is a mess."

"What?" Paul asks.

Anna waves her arms. "The room. The house." She looks at me. "Everything. We should have stayed in the apartment." Tears gather in her eyes.

I have no answer because she is right. "I'm sorry," I say.

The room is darkening in the late afternoon. It is a room without electricity, a room cluttered with ladders, saws, tools whose names I do not know. Electrical wires protrude like pigtails from the walls. We have taken two groups of strangers, crammed them into a small space, and tried to call them family. How could I have imagined it would work?

The buzzer sounds on the roaster, and I head to the bedroom to take out the cookies. Using a clean sock as a potholder, I set the cookie sheet to cool on some freshly laundered panties on the dresser. I pick up a T-shirt that says "Fresh Jive" and fold it.

Anna goes into the girls' room and shuts the door.

Paul comes into our room, bumps the cookie sheet, and spills cookies. "Oops," he says and takes a box of Ziplocs from a desk drawer. He blows the dust off the cookies and drops them into a bag.

I hear the front door open. "Hi, Mom." It's Brad. I hear him go into the kitchen and open the refrigerator. I start marking time, listening for the fridge to close.

I take cookie dough from the bowl on my desk, roll it into one-inch balls, and refill the cookie sheet.

"Here," I say to Paul. "Put your thumbprint on these cookies." I press his thumb into the first one.

I have not heard the refrigerator close. I know Paul is counting seconds too. He cannot fathom why my sons stare into an open fridge. When he has pressed his thumb into every ball of dough, I set the cookie sheet into the roaster and set the timer.

Paul clears his throat. When I can stand it no longer, in the last second before I think Paul will speak, I call out, "Close the refrigerator, Brad."

"Why does he do that?" Paul asks.

I shrug. "He's waiting for food to jump into his mouth."

Brad calls, "We got any cold pop?"

"Not anymore," Paul says.

Paul and I sit on the bed and fold clothes. The refrigerator closes. The front door opens.

Betsy calls, "Hi, Dad." She hurries into the girls' room, then into the bathroom. The shower comes on. Brad groans. He stands at our bedroom door now, raising his arms in a helpless gesture. "She beat me to the shower. I *need* a shower. She'll use all the hot water."

"You shouldn't have stared into the fridge so long," I say.

Brad stomps into the boys' bedroom.

"We need a new hot water heater," Paul says.

"Right," I say. "For all the fifty-gallon showers. And they use shampoo as if it flows from faucets."

I see Anna come out of the bedroom, leave the light on, and head for the kitchen. The refrigerator opens.

Now I am folding brassieres, tiny, teenage brassieres. "Does this serve a purpose?" I ask, holding one up to Paul.

Paul collapses on the bed, laughing. "And the way they *eat*," he says. "Eating machines. All of them."

I nod. "Have you noticed they use computers, but they can't turn off a light switch?"

Paul laughs again, and in spite of myself, I do too.

The cookie buzzer sounds. Brad comes back into our room and says, "What's up?" I hand him a cookie from the baggie.

Paul looks at me then at Brad, and says, "I'm taking your mother to Old Town. She needs a break."

I am pleased at this suggestion, but I say, "No, Paul. There isn't time."

Brad's eyes widen. "What about dinner? And hot water? I *need* a shower." He runs his fingers through his hair. "What will we eat for dinner?"

Paul reaches for his wallet, an action that calms Brad. "Here." Paul hands him some bills. "Take Anna and Betsy out for burgers. And Carter if you can find him."

"Burgers?" I say. "You don't give kids burgers on Christmas Eve."

"I do." Paul digs deeper in his wallet, hands Brad more money. "Have *good* burgers."

I gather a heap of socks and shove them into Paul's drawer. "There's no time for Old Town. There's laundry. And cookies. And we have to make a place to eat turkey in the warm part of the house." I imagine us eating Christmas dinner in our soon-to-be dining room, without a table, bundled in winter coats, sitting on folding chairs, balancing dinner plates on our knees.

Betsy comes out of the bathroom wrapped in a towel and slouches in our bedroom door.

"Betsy," Paul says. "Get your bathrobe."

"So we're going out for burgers?" She plants a hand on the curve of her hip and flips her dark, wet hair.

"Bathrobe." Paul points at her. "Now."

She ducks into her room.

Paul drops to his knees and begins to dig in the back of his closet. He drags out the Haliburton case and a tripod. "We'll photograph luminarias," he says. "Christmas lights on the square. And the church."

"Forget it," I say. "There isn't time."

Paul hands Brad the camera case and tripod saying, "Put these in the car." He knocks on the girls' door. "Betsy, fold these clothes. Anna, finish the cookies. Get everybody's thumbprint on those cookies."

No one protests. I'm amazed. Paul takes my arm and guides me toward the front door.

"So much to do," I say. "I'll be up all night." But even I can hear that my objections lack conviction.

We meet Carter coming in the front door.

"Carter," Paul says, "I'm taking your mother to Old Town. Brad has money for dinner. You kids clean this place up for tomorrow." He looks at me. "You need a coat." He looks at Carter. "Get her coat."

Carter rolls his eyes. "Do I look like the coat keeper?"

"Carter. Get it."

Carter brings my coat. Paul guides to me to the car.

Betsy, dressed now, stands in the front doorway. Brad waves. "So long, Mom. We've got it covered."

"Really, Paul," I say. "This isn't right."

Old Town is a tangle of slow-moving traffic and tour busses. Paul and I park four blocks off the plaza and walk. He carries the tripod. I hang the camera around my neck and pull my collar up against the cold.

"Look at the people," I say. "We can't fight this crowd." But when we round the last corner and step into the dark plaza, I have to catch my breath. Thousands of votive candles flicker inside brown paper bags. The little lights outline the streets, the rounded adobe buildings, the walkways. The night feels warmer here in the square, as if the lights have broken the chill.

As we step into the flow of foot traffic, I am struck by the silence. A hush has fallen. We cross the square and stand in front of the old church. I look into the open door, up the center aisle to the altar where a hundred candles flicker.

I prepare the camera, Paul opens the tripod, levels it, tightens the legs. I set the aperture and a slow shutter speed. Paul connects the cable to the shutter. I align a shot of a bell tower and buttress. A woman steps into the frame, then jumps back. "Sorry," she whispers.

I smile. "No problem. It's a long exposure."

Paul and I shoot several frames, bracketing shutter speeds.

Inside the church, a bell choir plays "Oh, Holy Night." I stand close against Paul. "I wish the kids were here."

"We'll bring them tomorrow. Tonight they're getting ready. Making it their Christmas too."

Paul takes the camera and tripod. "Let's walk."

We move east, down a narrow alley where mountains outline the sky and the moon casts backlight on the highest peaks. A yellow candle draws us to an alcove where, out of the chill, a shrine is built into an adobe wall.

"Oh!" I take a quick breath. "The Virgin of Guadalupe." Her life-sized figure floats in shades of warm ochre painted on adobe. Her eyes are closed, her hands folded. At her feet is an altar where candles flicker in clear glass.

I step closer. "She's so *peaceful*."

Paul smiles. "Even though she's a mother."

I chuckle softly. "Yes."

Paul slides his arm around my shoulders. I relax against him. We stand this way a long time.

Carols and Candles 11 P.M.

Roberta Goodwin

Greenview Hills Community Church, the sign says, although the building sits on a flat lawn in a flat block of Greenview Boulevard. There are no hills for miles, and the view across from the church's handkerchief of lawn is a row of small businesses. It's one of those church signs like a cafeteria menu, moveable white letters announcing sermon topics to come. Tonight it says only: Carols and Candles 11 P.M.

Mercury vapor lights arching above the street cast a glow that transforms the grass into an eerie spread of turquoise Astroturf. In the next block I can see a giant blue neon faucet dripping two huge drops and a splash onto the roof of Parnell's Plumbing. Two girls in leotards and leg warmers leave the Workout Station across the street. I wonder if the place ever closes. Otherwise the boulevard is quiet, the frenzied pack of shoppers finally gone home to stuff stockings.

But there is a glow coming from the amber windows of the church. I enter the lobby just as the choir marches down the center aisle singing "Angels We Have Heard on High." The church smell overcomes me. What is it? Musty hymnbooks, the clinging odor of a half-century of coffee grounds, a stale thrift shop smell that rises from the bags of castoff clothing perennially collected for the victims of catastrophes abroad, the sugary aroma of powdered donuts that are set out every Sunday after the service.

And there he is, the same smiling, peculiar usher who greets me every time I come here. Those occasions are few and far between: Easter once a decade; oftener, the Patriotic Service on the Fourth of July, when the church is strung with red, white, and blue crepe paper reminiscent of a small town in Iowa, when ice cream freezers lean against each other under the shade of the one tree that graces the Nursery School play yard. After the patriotic hymns have been exhausted, and stirring poems read, and the young people with guitars have performed "This Land Is Your Land, This Land Is My Land," the congregation picnics in the parking lot, where the smell of burning hamburger grease rises to heaven in a holy column, and those who have brought freezers of ice cream may eat free. Then, the usher wears navy blue slacks and a white shirt, and a Styrofoam imitation of a straw hat, with a red, white, and blue band.

Now he wears a wool suit and tie, but his smile is unchanged over all these years, in an unaltered round hopeful face. It seems as if he never ages, as if the meter hasn't been running.

"Merry Christmas," he whispers, and hands me a program. I take a seat at the back near a side aisle. I'm always poised to escape when I'm in a church. The light is low: dismally dim sconces line the walls; a chandelier hangs over the altar; there are two slanting many-armed candleholders, one slightly askew; two wispy live Christmas trees with small white lights. Poinsettias, of course, to flank the altar, where a matronly woman who has become minister since I was last here presides in a wine-colored robe.

She speaks of light and darkness and the Child that is born, her words accompanied by the choir's lulling responses. She reads us the Christmas story, but she is a modern minister and uses some new translation so that the familiar words are no longer familiar. We rise and sit, working our way through the list of carols on our programs. I take the opportunity to examine my fellow congregants. A young courting couple hold hands, she with a strange lopsided haircut and three rings in one ear. Elderly ladies you'd expect to be asleep at this hour. A handful of dutiful mild husbands. A man in a wheelchair in the center aisle. A young one who is surely a street person, in soiled and rumpled clothing, so nervous he can't sit still, wiggles and shifts and drums his fingers on his knee, and then suddenly falls asleep.

A row in front of me I recognize a mother I used to see at the nursery school, twenty years ago. Or was it fifty years ago, or six months? Somehow time has been suspended. This homely church sits on and on while the Workout Stations and TV Discount Marts come and go. Well, it's Christmas Eve and we are both alone, so I move forward and sit beside her and whisper, "Hello." She sings the alto part loudly as we labor through all the verses of "It Came Upon the Midnight Clear." She wears a rayon print dress stretched tightly over an enormous bosom; her hair is grey and lank, and she clutches a worn black purse.

The deacons are circulating now with their plates. The young man courting the girl with the rings in her ear drops in a twenty. The mother of the nursery school boy now six foot four and already losing his hair, turns toward me with a strange fixed smile and wide-open eyes and whispers, "I forgot my c'llection." I see her suddenly as a five-year-old with a dime tied in one corner of her little-girl hankie, which she has lost, or hidden, when the looming deacon comes for her offering.

Now that the business is over with, the lady minister launches into her homily. That's what the program calls it. I am half asleep now in the murmuring dim cave of the sanctuary, and dreaming about homilies. I thought that was something Catholic. What is a homily, anyway, a brief sermon? A homely sermon, homely humble homily, I wish I were home where a dictionary is. While I dream, the homily ends and the church begins to darken. The minister explains that it's all going except what she calls the Christ Light, one candle in the center of the altar. The deacons reappear to distribute candles in flimsy paper holders to each of us. Switches are flicked, choir members arise armed with snuffers, and the lights on the trees, the sconces, and those crooked rows of candles all go out. We sit silent in the embrace of a huge darkness.

Now, she explains, she will light one choir member's candle with the Christ Light. The choir members' candles are lit first, and two of them step down to pass their flames to the front row. Now in the dark the little lights spread like fireflies, perilously passed from row to row over shoulders. As they reach to the back of the church a pleasant glow arises, and we seem as close as a group of apemen in a warm cave, where shadows tremble on the high white ceiling. The flame has gotten to our row now, to an old lady wearing a green Christmas scarf and an ancient hat with a long curling feather. The candle passed over a shoulder to her wavers in its cardboard disk. I gasp: will the flame catch the corner of that scarf, mount up the fabric, releasing an acrid smell, then jump to the feather curling down, then to her hair? Who would save her? The mother next to me stares glassily at the aisle. Can the man in the wheelchair jockey his chair around, slap the flame with his program? The street person—could he push the chair aside and beat out the flames with his bare hands? No, he is still asleep.

But none of this happens. Someone nudges the street person awake, and he manages to light his candle, and I mine, and now everyone has a flame to hold. The choir starts off with "Silent Night," and we all sing, as they march back down the aisle and line up against the wall. Closest to me are two young men whose deep voices boom and drown out all the rest. We rise at last and drift toward the lobby, running out of verses and singing the first one over again.

The usher has a box for us to put our snuffed-out candles in, though now I don't want to give mine up. He can see this and he smiles his strange smile again, telling me, "You can have another next year."

At the door the minister wishes us Merry Christmas, and now it really is Christmas, twelve o'clock on Greenview Boulevard, and the married couples and courting couple head for the parking lot, someone pushes the wheelchair away, the elderly ladies are escorted off into the night. Merry Christmas, Merry Christmas, is all you can hear as the church is closed down. A lady from the choir turns back to hug the two young men who sang too loud, and her husband, standing next to me, confides: "I've been in a church maybe three, four times in my life. It's nothing but superstition." He snorts and jingles his car keys impatiently. And in that moment I lose sight of the glassy-eyed mother and the street person, who have both faded into the darkness of Christmas alone, as I too will, our brief connection snuffed out with the candles.

From the Kitchen of Julia Grissom

MRS. PAT NIXON'S HOT CHICKEN SALAD

4 cups cut up cooked chicken
2 tablespoons lemon juice
3/4 cup mayonnaise
1 teaspoon salt
2 cups chopped celery
4 hard-cooked eggs, sliced
3/4 cup cream of chicken soup
1 teaspoon finely minced onion
2 cans pimento, cut fine
1 1/2 cups crushed potato chips
1 cup grated cheese
2/3 cup finely chopped toasted almonds

Combine all ingredients except cheese, potato chips, and almonds. Place in a large rectangular baking dish. Top with cheese, potato chips, and almonds. Let stand overnight in refrigerator. Bake at 400 degrees F for 20 to 25 minutes. Makes 8 servings.

Remembrances

Clarence Stiles

Having lived in the early days of this century, we are steeped in the traditions of old-fashioned Christmases: cedar trees fresh from the forest, decorated with strings of popcorn, paper-ring ribbons, wax candles; and gifts of apples, oranges, hard candy, and sleds. We even hung stockings by the fireplace, hoping Santa would fill them with gifts when he came through the chimney. We yet hold with tradition when it comes to music, social graces, morality, prayer, marriage, and Christmas.

But when it comes to Christmas gifts we stray a bit. Today's "progress" dictates calculators, Nintendos, digital timepieces, cordless appliances, microwaves, VCRs, talking dolls, and so on.

In this day of computers, satellites, faxes, and lasers, we expect that soon (if not now possible) you will be able to feed our name and address into a computer and so program it that come Christmastime this mechanical brain (no heart) will spew out a "Christmas card," fold it into an envelope, affix a stamp, add our name and address, and call on Uncle Sam to deliver it to our door.

But, alas, then you will not even have to think of us. And that has been the beauty of the traditional greeting, that at least once a year you have us in your mind *and* heart.

Card Games

Suellen Wedmore

It's a week before Christmas, and greeting cards volley from household to household like Ping-Pong balls in a tournament. Aunt Matilda hurls one at us, and I fire one back to her in the next day's mail. The Card Game, I call it, ticking off addresses, scouring the town for gilt-edged angel stamps. And thinking back on thirty years I realize that—like every other game—this Yuletime shuffle has rules. Guidelines that help to order (and understand?) the chaos of this annual frenzy.

Rule #1—Procrastinate!

Always wait—as I did when my children were small—until at least mid-December before requesting a photo of your family for the yearly greeting card. My resulting film, when developed, did not contain one single picture where the entire family was smiling. In one photo the baby was howling, her fist pummeling the air, and in another finger-like horns sprouted mysteriously from behind my son's head.

"Did I do nothing but cry for five years?" my youngest asks now, on viewing these cards.

As the children grew older, I gave up the photo greetings in favor of purchased cards. *This year I'll get my cards out on time!* I promised.

This doesn't work, however, when you subscribe to the yard-is-always-greener-on-the-other-side-of-the-mall theory, as I do.

Sure, that card with the kitten peeking out of the red stocking was cute, but I was always sure a more exciting card was just around the corner.

On December 24, I was still turning corners.

Rule #2—Upgrade at Your Own Risk

One year I took a course in linoleum block printing because the teacher had promised in a cheery voice: "Make your own Christmas cards."

Big mistake!

This is like taking a course in gourmet cooking, which I also advise against. It changes the expectations of those around you. After *Paté de Campagne*, a bologna sandwich never quite looks the same.

For many years I spent the days before Christmas poised in front of a table laden with inks and rollers, cards drying on every horizontal surface of the house. These cards made it into the mail on December 23, and I was told many arrived at their destinations stuck to the envelopes because the ink was still wet.

Rule #3—Professional Is Not Always Better

Mass production is the answer! I decided several years ago. Create a simple sketch and have it professionally printed. Stick the copies in envelopes and be done with it!

Unfortunately, this idea conflicted with rule number one. Never mind that I'd had a long, balmy summer to sketch outdoors. December crept in and found me unprepared. And I drove around town for hours, in subzero weather, looking for the perfect scene for my Christmas card.

It's hard to capture the enhancement of a landscape when you're perched on the edge of a vinyl car seat, the steering wheel embedded in your chest.

Rule #4—Don't Cross Anyone off Your Christmas List

This rule dictates that if you eliminate anyone from your card list, they will immediately shoot a card to you in the next day's mail. Actually this is quite a useful rule once you understand it. Thus, if you really want to hear from someone, *don't* send them a card. This is one of those laws of nature that cannot be easily understood (like Bernoulli's law, which explains how the lower pressure of the air rushing over a plane's wing supports your Boeing 747 all the way to Albuquerque). You don't believe it but you accept it.

Rule #5—Include a Message of Some Kind

I received a card last year postmarked Suffolk, England, signed *Karen*.

This is contrary to Christmas card etiquette. Karen could have inherited a fortune, married Prince Charles (who I hear is more or less available), or sold her romance novel to Aardvark Publishing. But all I know for sure is that she's alive and can remember her name.

Christmas cards are long-distance gossip. Tell your correspondent something new about yourself. Fair is fair.

Rule #6—Forget the Display

This rule is counter to the myth that your hard work will be rewarded when you display all the lovely cards you receive from others. It's been my experience that Christmas cards have a mind of their own, and that absolutely nothing will hold them in place like the displays you see in *Woman's Day*.

Masking tape dries out as soon as you attach it to the cards; Scotch tape peels off the door frame, taking the enamel with it. And the mastic gum they sell in hardware stores clings to everything else—your sweater, the chicken breasts on the counter thawing—but pops from the wall within an hour of application.

Set a reasonable goal—say displaying 50 percent of the cards you receive. The others will find their way into the yard or into the laundry with the colored washables. But those that remain—those cherubs with the secret smiles, the wolves with snow covering their heads like frosty dandruff—make it all worthwhile.

As for reward: there's the handwritten messages from your friends and relatives to inspire you for another year!

Yes, I'm sure of it now. Karen is having an affair with Prince Charles.

From the Kitchen of Suellen Wedmore

AFTER-THE-HOLIDAYS SAN FRANCISCO STREETCAR EXPRESS

8 slices raisin bread, toasted

1 pound asparagus, boiled until tender (or one can asparagus)

8 slices leftover turkey breast

8 slices baked or boiled ham

Sauce

1 3/4 cups milk (may use low-fat or skim)

8 tablespoons flour

1 stick margarine (may use 1/2 low-fat butter substitute)

1 3/4 cup grated sharp cheddar cheese (may use low-fat)

1/8 teaspoon dry mustard

Fresh ground pepper to taste

Paprika for garnish as desired

Place toast on a cookie sheet covered with aluminum foil (for easy cleaning). Top with sliced turkey breast, sliced ham, and 2 or 3 spears of asparagus for each open-faced sandwich.

For sauce, heat the margarine in a heavy sauce pan and stir in the flour slowly using a whisk. Slowly add the milk and whisk until it thickens. Add 1 1/2 cups grated cheese, pepper, and dry mustard. Taste and adjust flavors. The sauce should be as thick as whipped cream. Using a spoon, place the sauce in dollops on top of each open sandwich. Top with the extra 1/4 cup grated cheese. Put under the broiler until the sauce is puffed and brown, about 10 minutes. Sprinkle with paprika and serve hot.

The Search for the Perfect Tree

Shanna Eilers

It's a pleasant, wet, and rainy day in Bothell, and I am standing in a semicircle of approximately 133 "you cut 'em" Christmas trees.

My husband is running with a saw blade in his left hand, a blue tarp in his right hand, and a translucent look in his eyes. Evidently, he has spotted yet another tree that might meet his specific conditions.

My seven-year-old daughter is lying on the ground at my feet, moaning deliriously that she is "tree sick." Her tiny limp body is lying quietly as she explains that after rows and rows of trees she can no longer muster the energy to walk another step.

I don't know about you, but when I go to "cut 'em" I don't waste a lot of time. I stride briskly to the most attractive tree standing and shout, "Here!"

Your professional Christmas tree cutter (husband), on the other hand, does not even think about cutting until he has conducted a complete tree study of the site—circling the selected tree warily, as though it were an alien spaceship, checking it out from every possible angle, squinting and squatting; checking the wind, feeling the needles, analyzing the distance from the road to the truck, back to the tree . . .

And so, amid an atmosphere of unbearable tension, comparable to not being able to find your car keys when you are already late to that very important meeting, my daughter and I wait, and wait, and wait.

By now our daughter is trying to make snow angels in the mud, and I am unbelievably letting her. I see other families in the tree farm. They're staring intently at trees way off in the distance, but I think they're staring at us. We have been here so long.

I think about grabbing my daughter's hand and pulling her up to her feet and taking her down the hill for our third cup of hot cider and her second candy cane, but too late, she has been entertaining the crowds by holding her breath as she runs up and down the tree rows.

The more time that passes with virtually nothing happening, the more excited I get about that cider. I start down the hill when suddenly I hear a loud, long, whopping yelp that I recognize as my husband.

I turn to see him stand up, wipe tree pitch off his hands, and in a voice that would make a gold digger stop, announce, "This . . . is the tree." There it stands in all of its glory—all fourteen feet of it.

"That's too big," I say.

"Not so," he says. "I will trim off the bottom. You'll see."

"Don't you remember last year?" I ask. "It was too big; you didn't trim enough."

"Did so."

"Did not."

"Did so."

"Did."

"Not!"

Like anything else, success depends on the proper tools, so in the back of our car is an assortment of many saws, blue tarps, gloves, rope, and any necessity to fell Paul Bunyan's tree.

"Quick, run back to the car and pick out the yellow-handled two-blade milliliter saw. Oh, and by the way, grab me a cider," he says with a big smile.

Rolling my eyes back in my head and shrugging my shoulders, I approach the tree surgeon, punch him in the arm where he pretends to be knocked into the fir tree, and head to the car trying to consider the many, many complex factors involved in the "you cut 'em" tree man.

This is, after all, a once a year experience. And this tree—prepare to experience a heart tremor—is home-cut. How are we ever going to get it on the car, let alone through the front door? At least when I finally do get home I can make a nice hot cup of apple cider.

From the Kitchen of Shanna Eilers

HOT SPICY APPLE CIDER

6 cups apple cider
1 cinnamon stick
1/4 cup honey
1/4 teaspoon nutmeg
3 tablespoons lemon juice
l teaspoon lemon rind
1 can (2 1/2 cups) unsweetened pineapple juice

Heat cider and cinnamon stick in a large pan. Bring to a boil and simmer covered for 5 minutes. Add remaining ingredients and simmer uncovered for 5 minutes longer.

SIMPLY DELICIOUS EGGNOG

1 egg
2 tablespoons sugar
1 cup milk, chilled
1/4 teaspoon vanilla

Beat egg and sugar together. Beat in milk and vanilla. Serve cold in a tall glass sprinkled lightly with nutmeg.

The Goody Boxes

Toni Wood

My mother believes that if you care about someone, you feed them. And if you *really* love someone, you feed them something extraordinarily rich. On Christmas morning, we traditionally find Mom's "goody boxes" under the tree, one for each of her children, one for each spouse, one for each grandchild. Thirteen goody boxes in all. Enough cookies and candy so that we can gorge ourselves publicly and privately for days.

Last year each of us hinted it might be time to change this tradition—waistlines, health reasons, that sort of thing. Mom took offense. What sort of logic was this? Did we mean to take all the fun out of Christmas? Where had she gone wrong, to raise such joyless children?

Christmas Eve, we gathered in Mom and Dad's big house, but the familiar smells did not greet us. The kitchen table was bare. No divinity, no "hello dollies," no fudge, no fried walnuts cooling on wax paper. No sign of my favorite cookies with the chow mein noodles and butterscotch chips. No sign of my sister's beloved "brown candy," made of boiled sugar and cream. No half-filled boxes in the corner. We did see goody boxes under the tree, so we thought Mom was just unusually organized.

Christmas morning, during a frenzy of unwrapping, with paper flying and children screeching, we each opened our goody boxes to find . . . carrots!

We laughed. We congratulated Mom. "Well it's about time," we said.

And we tried to be brave. But the rest of the day didn't seem quite right. We stuffed ourselves with turkey and mashed potatoes and yeast rolls, but there was nothing sweet to top it off. The traditional card games and whooping dictionary game kept our attention. But none of us sneaked off to the back bedroom to pick through our boxes. In years past, when my brother and sister weren't looking, I liked to ransack their boxes and devour their chow mein noodle cookies. But there was nothing to pick through. Throughout the evening we munched on popcorn and, of all things, apple slices.

My sister was the first to complain. She did it quietly.

"I want my brown candy," she said. She was surly after losing a round of continental rummy.

"I want something chocolate," my brother said.

"Ha!" my mother answered, triumphant. "There will be no goodies this year in my house. Let them eat carrots!"

I wandered into the kitchen and poked through the tightly packed cabinets.

"Don't you even have the ingredients for chow mein cookies? Don't you have any butterscotch chips? I'll make them myself."

"No, I don't have the ingredients," Mom said. "And get out of my cabinets."

My brother went to the phone and dialed the town's only supermarket. Closed. He called the quick-stop markets. Closed for Christmas.

We gave up.

The day after Christmas is traditionally my mother's day. She takes one of her brand new mysteries that my father gives her and sits in the easy chair to read all day. No one, not even a grandchild, is allowed to ask for a meal, a drink, or a clean towel.

But last year, on the morning after Christmas, before we were even dressed, Mom drove to the IGA and filled her shopping cart. Coconut, chocolate, pecans, walnuts, butterscotch chips, cream, a few pounds of sugar. By 9 A.M. she started baking, and by early afternoon we were afloat in rich cookies and candy.

We cheered her on, fighting each other to fill our goody boxes, because we knew that on this day after Christmas, Mom was showing she *really* loved us.

From the Kitchen of Toni Wood

PEANUT BUTTERSCOTCH CRUNCHIES

1/2 cup peanut butter
1 (6-ounce) package butterscotch chips
1 (3-ounce) can chow mein noodles

Combine peanut butter and butterscotch chips in top of double boiler. Place over hot (not boiling) water until butterscotch melts. Stir until blended. Add chow mein noodles and stir until well coated. Drop teaspoonfuls onto waxed paper-lined cookie sheet. Chill until set.

The Mints Maker, Times Three

Ruth Moose

Brother and I
watch father at the stove
magician's elbows out
he measures water
holds to light, scoops
sugar and stirs.
A special pan
and cup and wooden spoon
the glass testing rod
always exact and upright.

He cuts butter
palms pressed so fast
only the secret is safe
and the spoon swirls
in a rhyme of metal, metal,
wooden oar.

In the silver circle
heat rises bubbles hiss
and break. A burst
of crystal flowers.
He spins
a glass thread
and tastes his finger,

pours the hot puddle
onto cold marble
buttered on the winter
porch.

A night
in mid-December
we wait for Christmas
and the spreading pool
of our faces thickens
around the cooling shore.

He ruffles the edges,
flutes the crystal crust.
A round window
he wipes our eyes
the extract stings
in our breathing cold.

When the glass
is cool enough
his hands tough
and hard and ready
he pulls the twisted hank
into silk, spins
the stretching rope,
slaps it back into itself.
Loop and back again.
The rope is a noose,

a lasso, an arm, a fat
taffy fist.
The art is smooth
and patient as he pulls
sugar into silk,
silk into rope
the thin shine
a ribbon of wonder.

We find
and oil the scissors,
obedient bird
wants to race
the striped snake
onto paper waxed in green
and red foil tins.

Three days
the nuggets cream
to magic. They taste
of mint and sugar
and my father's hands.
The gift he gave
from a Christmas
heart that earned
him fifty-seven years
and a memory
that melts for me
like nothing else.

From the Kitchen of Ruth Moose

DADDY'S PULLED MINTS

3 cups granulated sugar
1/2 stick *real* butter (no substitute)
1 cup boiling water
Oil of peppermint
Food coloring, red and green

Measure sugar into saucepan. Cut butter into pats atop it. Add boiling water. Stir with a wooden spoon. Once the mixture reaches a rolling boil, *do not stir again.* Cook until candy thermometer reaches 260 degrees F. Pour onto a cold marble slab. (Chill the slab in a freezer several hours or leave outside in winter weather so it is cold through and through.)

Drop 10 or 12 drops of oil of peppermint and 5 or 6 drops of desired Christmas color onto the candy.

When candy has cooled enough to handle, thickly butter palms of both hands, divide the mixture in half, and pull like taffy. (You need a partner taking the other half.) Pulling takes practice and skill. You pull until your arms ache. You pull and loop the rope of candy until it loses its sheen. Stretch it into a thin ribbon, and with oiled scissors, cut the candy into bite-sized pieces onto waxed paper. Let the mints cream three days in a very cool place.

This recipe makes 1 1/2 pounds of mints that truly melt in your mouth.

Warning: This recipe is *not* to be tackled by the faint-hearted and can only be made when the weather is *very* cold, the sky is *very* clear, and the air is *very* crisp. Weather greatly affects the outcome. Practice and patience make a skilled candy maker.

It's New, It's Improved, It's Christmas

Bob Rhubart

The holidays are a time of rituals. Some of these, like the shopping, the music, the decorations, and the food, are comforting in their predictability. Other rituals, like the shopping, the music, the decorations, and the food, can leave you curled into the fetal position in some dark corner, whimpering. How you react to these various rituals depends a lot on your general disposition and credit card balance. I, for one, love Christmas. But there is one Christmas ritual that really tangles my tinsel: the seasonal editorializing about how our modern celebration of the holidays pales in comparison to that of Christmas past.

It's not that the old notions of how to celebrate the holidays aren't all cozy and romantic—you can't watch marathon broadcasts of *It's a Wonderful White Christmas Carol on Thirty-Fourth Street* without a nostalgic teardrop or two falling onto your plate of Christmas nachos. It's just that the loudest cheerleaders for "old-fashioned" holiday celebrations are overlooking the fact that way-back-when those people didn't have the option of doing it any other way.

Dashing through the snow in a one-horse open sleigh? No thanks. When Christmas morning rolls around, I'm going to be mighty grateful that the family is going to hop into a nice warm Toyota for the ride over to Grandma's place. I figure a horse-drawn sleigh is big fun for maybe fifteen minutes. After that you're going to want Old Dobbin to haul ass back to someplace warm where the eggnog is spiked and the family can gather in the flickering glow of a giant TV and contemplate the true meaning of football.

Chestnuts roasting on an open fire? Sorry. No fireplace. We've got a furnace for heat, and stuffing nuts in there voids the warranty. Any of the roasting we do these days is in the microwave, and I'm pretty sure that if you put chestnuts in the microwave they would become little Yuletide hand grenades. Although, if you've got a snoot full of Yule grog, watching chestnuts explode in your microwave might be a real hoot. Some people may see microwave ovens as a symptom of creeping nontraditional holiday-ism. But I'll bet you that if there were microwave ovens around in Charles Dickens' day, the Cratchits wouldn't have had to entertain an uncharacteristically giddy Scrooge for six or seven hours while the turkey cooked.

Holiday entertaining is, in fact, the one area that even the most severe critic of modern practices would have to admit has not changed since Tim was Tiny. A good holiday celebration, then as now, involves lots of food, free-flowing drink, and a gathering of friends and family, some of whom you are about as happy to see as a subpoena. Just as the Cratchits' Christmas was spent with a man who, for all they knew, had suffered some kind of head trauma, so the modern holiday gathering includes relatives or acquaintances who, because they watch too many talk shows, and/or have poor personal hygiene, and/or fail to maintain scheduled medication, you would normally avoid like a plate of frosted botulism. But in the season of good will toward all, you smile warmly at the mystery uncle wandering around half-crocked with a clump of mistletoe dangling from the bill of his NRA cap.

Dickens' story wouldn't have become the holiday classic it has if, having spotted on their doorstep an insanely grinning, raw-poultry-bearing, fresh-off-a-rough-night Scrooge, the Cratchits had pulled their shades and pretended not to be home. Which is probably what I would have done. Instead, knowing full well his reputation as a career grouch, they welcomed him into their home, and we have a touching story that teaches a valuable lesson about how the Christmas spirit can get the boss to pump up the payroll.

Despite what the critics might say, our modern Christmas isn't all that different from those of long ago. Sure the technology has changed, but that just means a bigger, brighter, louder Christmas, with lasers and holograms and stuff. It's our modern celebration of a season that even the least spiritual among us recognizes as a time of hope that the nutcases of the world will wake up and realize that peace on earth is a win-win proposition for everybody. If Christmas has changed, it's for the better. We should continue making Christmas bigger and louder and shinier until everybody gets it.

It's Time for the Doldrums

Jan Epton Seale

Certain things before Christmas cry to be mentioned: holly wreaths, manger scenes, goodwill. The time after Christmas furnishes its own list of tearjerkers.

In many of us, a postholiday fit of ill will can be induced by the necessity of cleaning the turkey. Nutritionists tout a turkey's wonderful protein worth, but a turkey is still ten pounds of high quality succulent meat stuck together with ten pounds of slimy ligaments, dagger tendons, and enough grease to lubricate a wagon train.

Lurking in my background somewhere is the Puritan duty to sit down with an old bird carcass and pick off every smidgen of meat, presumably to make those alliterative recipes like Turkey Tetrazzini. My mother even boils the carcass after the picking, claiming it delivers tasty soup broth. I'm sorry, Mom, but some family traditions are just not worth preserving. When the "inner basting" has worked its way to my elbows, I quit. I'm not really big on being a link in the food chain.

Then there's always some soggy leftover dressing inside the bird. No one has ever, as far as I'm concerned, been able to come up with a decent recipe using leftover dressing. Dressing is a casserole, and mixing a casserole into another casserole amounts to the same thing as mixing all the colors: you get grey.

Taking the tree down also produces a lot of anti-Christian behavior at our house. The world is divided into two groups of tree-takers-down: those who look on a December 26 tree as criminal evidence to be disposed of as quickly and discreetly as possible, and those who insist the tree must stay up until the second week in January because it's so expensive.

We are in Group One, and so, on the morning of December 26, the tree is hastily undressed and hauled to the alley, usually with a small boy riding it. Meanwhile, back in the house, I begin vacuuming the swath of dead needles and foil icicles while the dog sits nibbling the imbedded glitter in her paw.

What really brings on the muttering is to find, after the stars and elves and angels have gone to their respective small boxes and all those put into one big box labeled Xmas Decor and this big box heaved to the top shelf in the utility room—what really makes me see red is to find we left out the doorknob cozy Aunt Lilly knitted for us seven years ago, or to notice a little Santa cup ho-ho-ho-ing on the counter.

Close following is the onset of mechanical mayhem. The true nature of gift toys and small appliances becomes apparent. Batteries die. Plastic dinosaurs suddenly cease ranging over the earth. We begin roaming through the discarded boxes, seeking warranty cards and assembly directions. And we realize we are never going to win a game of brain teasers our sons bought us.

We tell ourselves to be philosophical, to understand that mountaintop experiences are possible only because there are valleys between.

And then we secretly thank God for the eleven quiet months ahead before the next orgy of human-designed folderol.

December 26

Barbara Bolz

It's not Christmas day you look forward to, but the day after Christmas when all of the wrapping paper has been thrown out and the gifts placed proudly in their new homes; when everyone plays Monopoly, drinks ginger ale, and eats turkey sandwiches with Grandma's special cranberry sauce condiment, and then tops it off with Auntie Ann's Christmas bread pudding. It's the day when there isn't much to do but sit on the couch and look at each other.

There's your sister Nadia. Named Lisa at birth, she changed it to Nadia when she turned eighteen. After tattooing and piercing various parts of herself, she really shocked everyone by marrying a Lutheran minister last fall. You've a hunch they'll be bringing a baby next Christmas to swell the ranks of the youngest generation. And there's your brother Gary, playing the piano composition he wrote years ago. Not for the first time, you notice how your father doesn't seem capable of hearing it too often. And Mom and Dad, after decades of ups and downs and trials and joys, they seem as solid as possible. You adore them for weathering all the storms without allowing their marriage to capsize. Grandmother is sitting in the corner, fidgeting with her purse as she watches the festivities. Will the lifelong teetotaler take a sip of mulled Christmas wine this year, you wonder? And Grandfather's next to her, telling the children about the enormous "golly whopper" of a zucchini he grew last summer. His hands are stretched as far as they will go and the children watching have equally widened eyes. The younger ones shudder at the thought of having to eat such a large vegetable, but the older ones know he's stretching it; they also know that by listening, they're assured of an ice cream cone later.

As you watch your children and their cousins playing with the new treasures, you realize in a flash (why hadn't you thought of it before?) that you aren't on the floor with them. You are no longer of *that* generation, the generation that makes Christmas worth putting on each year. You've taken over your parent's role, and now you are making Christmas happen by baking, decorating, writing notes to Santa, and reading *The Night*

Before Christmas just before the kids go to bed. Suddenly, you look over at your mom and dad and realize that they're the grandparents now. They *are* older, aren't they? When did it happen? You think of how these very same thoughts must have occurred to your mother and to your grandmother, to *her* mother and her grandmother, and on and on, back through all the generations recorded in your leather-bound family Bible. Each of these women in turn must have stood in their living rooms on the day after Christmas, thinking these very same thoughts.

And what holds together all of the generations parading on? As the Fiddler on the Roof might say, "Tradition!" Nobody in your family knows exactly why they roast chestnuts on an open fire or place a tree in the corner of the living room each December, but they do these things nevertheless, knowing that if they didn't, something dreadful might happen. The year you wished to explain the metaphysical significance of indoor greenery during the darkest and coldest time of the year, everyone was much more interested in finding Aunt Teresa's cross-stitched ornament: "The one she made about ten years ago, you know, with the mouse popping out of a Christmas stocking." No, we don't need to know why we do the same things year after year to be beholden to those traditions. It's enough simply to do them and to keep doing them, knowing that one day those young ones playing on the floor will make Christmas magical for their own children. For the truth of the holiday season, the truth you understand as you watch your family and as they watch you, is that we belong to each other. We belong to our children as much as they belong to us. We *belong* to our mothers and fathers, our aunts and uncles, our grandparents and nieces and nephews. And each Christmas, as we give gifts to those we love, we are reminding them of this truth, saying, "Take a little part of me—this wall hanging I've made or this book I've saved—take it as a sign that you have the rest of me as well."

From the Kitchen of Barbara Bolz

AUNTIE ANN'S CHRISTMAS BREAD PUDDING

6 cups cubed, dried, leftover bread

2 cups whole milk

2 cups cream

1 cup raisins

1 cup shredded sweetened coconut

1 1/2 cups chopped pecans

1 cup mixed dried fruit

1 tablespoon cinnamon

1 teaspoon nutmeg

4 eggs, beaten

6 tablespoons melted butter

2 tablespoons vanilla

Preheat oven to 350 degrees F. Combine all ingredients in a bowl until moist. Pour into a buttered dish and cook for one hour. Serve warm, covered with hard sauce.

HARD SAUCE FOR BREAD PUDDING

1 stick of butter

1 egg

1 1/2 cups powdered sugar

1/2 cup of whiskey

Cream butter and sugar together over medium heat. Remove from heat and blend in egg. Pour whiskey into the mixture, stirring continually.

One nice thing about going home is that
you don't have to make a reservation.

—C.E. McKenzie

That Moment

Pat Schneider

Strange how they come home and for days there is a cyclone in the house—a good, wonderful twister of disorientation: color and light and laughter and food, the old games of teasing played again for remembrance and for intimacy across the chasms of their now different lives—and as suddenly they are gone again. Then something in the ornaments hurts the heart, so that immediately the tree, the lights, the crèche must all come down, be packed away. How good then, the clean floors, the dusted rooms, the stillness in the house. Because in that clean, clear space, their laughter tumbles in the silence; the shapes of their bodies relaxed around a game of crazy eights lingers in the space in the living room like a kind of transparency, and it blesses, as if that enduring, that abiding, that memory, is after all the great treasure. Not the cyclone itself, exciting though that was, but the deep calm after the storm, in which a strange light breaks over everything and everything is revealed as the spirit of itself, perfect, centered, and everlasting. That moment when the child at the kitchen table turns toward her grandmother, laughing, saying, "Grandma, I love you." That moment, for example, forever.

Taking Down the Tree

Anita Skeen

On January 5, everyone in the house
gone, I wrap the glass balls in pieces
of old socks as my mother taught me.
The tiny wooden chair, a private symbol
of grief, goes in the carton near Patrick's
glass cat and the red metal trikes and sleds
get parked in the last compartment.
When I unwrap the strands of lights,
spiraling like memories, I wind them
in neat wreaths, as my father taught me,
return them to their cellophane packs.
This tree was dead before its time.
The tiny knives slide under my nails,
attack my palms. I try to be gentle
with brittle branches, not snapping them
as I unclip the lamps, though I know
they are destined for mulch and flame.

From the tape deck, voices
of the Cincinnati Women's Choir,
"Music in My Mother's House," fill the room.
I glance out the window at the new wind chimes,
green with tinsel stripes like candy canes,
frantic in the chaotic weather.
What did it sound like before this gift?
I wonder, and think how they take me back

to something I can't name, some place
where small, delicate chambers bump together
in lost time, aiming peculiar notes
my way. "O Tannebaum, O Tannebaum,"
the chimes sing out. I see the choir,
a forest of voices in their green robes,
notes exploding among them
like colored lights.

A Recipe for Successful Holidays

Eunice Holtz

Storytelling around the dinner table is one of the most enjoyable happenings at our holidays. Most of my family would say they are not storytellers, but for the past two decades we have used a delightful method that invites everyone to share a memory. We make up slips with questions or unfinished statements. Each person is assigned one or chooses one to talk about.

Children enjoy listening to the stories of the adults as much as the grown-ups appreciate learning of the experiences that have impressed the children. The sharing of memories usually brings forth chuckles and enriches our lives as we mull over the stories later.

Here is our list. Use it or make up questions pertinent to your family.

1. On my first day at school, I remember . . . .

2. One of the hardest (or most embarrassing) things for me to do as a child was . . . .

3. As a child, my favorite hiding place was . . . .

4. When I was learning to drive a car . . . .

5. When I was a child, summer was a time to (share a favorite summer activity) . . . .

6. Recess in grade school meant time to play (name games and activities) . . . .

7. I remember getting a scolding for . . . .

8. One of my favorite holiday memories is of . . . .

9. An especially pleasant scene from my childhood days was . . . .

10. Sunday was special at my house when I was a child because . . . .

11. One thing I was allowed to do as a child that seemed special was . . . .

12. I laugh at myself when remembering the time I . . . .

13. A song that was popular when I went on my first date (or other special occasion) was . . . .

14. One of the most mischievous things I did in my childhood was . . . .

15. One food that brings back memories of my childhood is . . . .

16. The spookiest place in or around my childhood home was . . . .

17. When I think back to the night sounds in my childhood home, I remember . . . .

18. An aroma that brings back memories of childhood is . . . .

19. The pets I remember from my childhood were . . . .

20. One of the special people I remember is . . . .

Someone said, "Life is not marked by days and hours, but by memories." Enjoy the memories.

Contributors

KAREN ACKLAND lives in Santa Cruz, California, with her husband. As a Marketing Manager she usually writes in bulleted sentence fragments, a style not entirely avoided in this piece. She was previously published in *The Book Group Book* anthology.

KARREN L. ALENIER is the author of three collections of poetry including *Bumper Cars: Gertrude Said She Took Him for a Ride*. She recently completed a libretto about the life and work of Gertrude Stein. She is president of The Word Works, a small press publishing contemporary poetry in collectors editions.

CAROL BARRETT is on the faculty of The Union Institute in Cincinnati. Her poems appear in over eighty literary magazines and a variety of anthologies. In 1991 she received a creative writing fellowship from the National Endowment for the Arts.

JEAN BLACKMON is a columnist and short story writer with children, stepchildren, and grandchildren. She lives in Corrales, New Mexico, with her husband, John Waszak, who likes to remodel their house. Her work has appeared in publications such as the *Dallas Morning News* and *Tumblewords: Writers Reading the West*.

MARILYN J. BOE lives in Bloomington, Minnesota, with her husband, Bill. She writes poetry in a Scandinavian-styled hut in her backyard. Her work has appeared in *Loonfeather, Sidewalks, Passages North, Poetry East, Poets On:*, among others and in numerous anthologies.

BARBARA BOLZ writes, teaches, and enjoys being a mother in Ellettsville, Indiana, where she lives with her companion, Kath Pennavaria, and their son, Adam. She received her PhD in English from Indiana University and now runs Heirloom Biographies, a business that provides biographies for ordinary people.

SUZANNE C. COLE taught English at Houston Community College for many years and has published college textbooks, articles, essays, and poetry. Her book *To Our Heart's Content: Meditations for Women Turning 50* was published by Contemporary Books in May 1997.

CHARLOTTE A. COTÉ, a native Nebraskan, moved to Wisconsin in her midtwenties, married, raised four children, and received her MA from the University of Wisconsin, Milwaukee. She published the biography of noted feminist Olympia Brown and a 150-year history of a Racine, Wisconsin, church. She has received several poetry awards and continues to write poetry, nonfiction, and fiction.

BARBARA CROOKER has published nearly 600 poems in magazines such as *Yankee, The Christian Science Monitor, Country Journal,* in more than fifty anthologies (including five from Papier-Mache), and in five books. She has received three Pennsylvania Council on the Arts Fellowships in Literature, and is very thankful for her wonderful husband, three children, and son-in-law (her oldest was a recent bride).

PAMELA DITCHOFF: mix a shy, religious mother with a playful, ambitious father; add lots of love and simmer over a warm hearth in the Midwest. Stir in a big pencil and fine teachers, season with imagination, and wait. After three children are born, add poetry and a masters degree. Bring soup to a boil by adding *Bread Loaf, Papier-Mache,* several publications, and a first novel. The Pamela soup took forty-six years to make; I hope you find it worth the wait.

JULIA TAYLOR EBEL'S writings reflect her interest in family and nature. She is a private tutor, community college instructor, and advocate of reading with children. A mother of two college-age sons, she and her husband live in Jamestown, North Carolina.

SHANNA EILERS, a Seattle native, pens a local food column, "Overdone and Undercooked." Her regrets are that cereal hardens in the bowl and that her gums are receding. Her pleasure is her best friend, Rob (husband), and their teenage daughter, Braiden, who verbally challenges each home-cooked meal with, "Can't we eat out?"

BLANCHE FLANDERS FARLEY is a special collections librarian in Atlanta, Georgia. Her poems and stories have appeared in numerous journals and anthologies. She is coeditor of *Like a Summer Peace: Sunbright Poems and Old Southern Recipes* (Papier-Mache Press).

JULIA FISHER, based in Oak Park, Illinois, is a public relations consultant, patient advocate, and former college English teacher. In 1990 when her husband was diagnosed with a brain tumor, Julia became his advocate, learning far more than she wanted to know about the medical system.

LINDA ANN FORD, born and raised in East Cambridge, Massachusetts, lives in Santa Cruz, California. "I happily reside with my love, Tim, and our three cats. I'd like to dedicate this story to my parents, Elizabeth and Nick Geraigery."

LINDA NEMEC FOSTER's poems have appeared in numerous magazines and journals including, *The Georgia Review, Mid-American Review, Nimrod,* and *Quarterly West.* She authored three chapbooks; her first full-length collection of poems, *Living in the Fire Nest* (Ridgeway Press), was nominated for the Small Press Book Award in Poetry. In 1996 she received the prestigious poetry fellowship from the Arts Foundation of Michigan. Her work appeared in *I Am Becoming the Woman I've Wanted* (Papier-Mache Press).

HELEN FRIEDLAND has a BA in Economics from New York University, and an MA from Columbia University. Her published work includes poems, a children's book in rhyme, and articles in professional journals on the socioeconomic impact of industrial pollution.

MICHAEL S. GLASER serves as chair of the English Department at St. Mary's College of Maryland where he also directs the annual Literary Festival at St. Mary's. He has published over 200 poems in literary journals, anthologies, and newspapers. His chapbook, *In the Men's Room and Other Poems,* was the winner of the 1996 Painted Bride Quarterly Chapbook competition.

ROBERTA GOODWIN is a Virginian living in Los Angeles, where she indexes books, edits, writes, and enjoys the jazz scene. Her poems and stories have appeared in several publications, including *The Christian Science Monitor, Parting Gifts,* and *Piedmont Literary Review.*

CAPPY LOVE HANSON, a California native, writing junkie, and snowboarder, lives north of Santa Fe, New Mexico, with a lot of plants and a small parrot. Her work has appeared in such diverse publications as *Writer's Digest, Blue Mesa Review,* and *The New Mexican.*

JANICE J. HEISS is a San Francisco writer and performer. In the 1980s, she performed standup comedy and performance art at clubs and theaters throughout the Bay Area. She was also a member of the theater troupe, The Plutonium Players. Her prose and poetry have been published in numerous publications including, *Jewish Currents, Androgyne,* and *Herotica 2* (under a pseudonym).

EUNICE HOLTZ lives in Madison, Wisconsin, where she is a member of the Wisconsin Fellowship of Poets and has had her poems published in the WFOP yearly calendars. She says "Home for the Holidays" means time for sharing family stories with three children and five grandsons.

MEG HUBER grew up in Ann Arbor, Michigan, in a faculty family of musicians and writers. She graduated from Indiana University where she learned to admire good writing in its many forms. Her poetry has been published in a variety of periodicals, but this is her first prose submission.

SHIRLEY VOGLER MEISTER—an award-winning Indianapolis author whose prose and poetry have appeared in diverse U.S. and Canadian publications—has poems in four other Papier-Mache anthologies: *When I Am an Old Woman I Shall Wear Purple*, *If I Had My Life to Live Over I Would Pick More Daisies*, *I Am Becoming the Woman I've Wanted*, and *Grow Old Along with Me-The Best Is Yet to Be*.

MELISSA MILICH is a former newspaper columnist and has published numerous short stories, articles, and essays. She is the author of two children's books, including *Miz Fannie Mae's Fine New Easter Hat* (Little, Brown) and *Can't Scare Me!* (Doubleday). She is currently working on revisions for her first adult novel, to be published by Simon & Schuster.

S. MINANEL—thanks to her work appearing in Papier-Mache Press anthologies and other publications—is listed in the eighth edition of the *International Who's Who in Poetry and Poets' Encyclopeadia* published by the International Biographical Centre of England. She is thrilled that the same centre, after careful perusal of all her credentials, has nominated her "International Man of the Year."

RUTH MOOSE has published in *Atlantic Monthly, Redbook, Ladies' Home Journal, Yankee,* and other places. She is the author of two books of short stories: *The Wreath Ribbon Quilt* and *Dreaming in Color* published by August House. Her work appeared in *I Am Becoming the Woman I've Wanted* (Papier-Mache Press). She teaches creative writing at the University of North Carolina at Chapel Hill.

EILEEN MURPHY is a fifteen-year-old writer from New York state who loves to write. "My <cough, cough> charming family is the source of a lot of my inspiration; I'm one of six kids. Aside from writing, I love art, my friends, and horseback riding (hunter jumpers). And I'm very open to publishers."

GAIL PICKUS was born in Chicago into a family where storytelling and a sense of humor were key. "Mother, a ballet dancer, and Dad, an artist, encouraged creativity. Marrying, moving to South Dakota, and raising three sons kept me laughing and telling stories."

MARY EILEEN PRICE was born in Kenton, Ohio, in 1922. Her first writing experience was a self-published cookbook, *Memories of Mama's Kitchens.* A member of Virginia Romance Writers and Romance Writers of America, her first novel *Love Me to Sleep Tonight,* was published in 1995.

BERNICE RENDRICK was born in Kansas in 1930 but has lived in California most of her life. She belongs to the Santa Cruz Writers' Union Poetry Group and participates in radio appearances, readings, and workshops. The group recently published the anthology *Coast Lines.*

BOB RHUBART lives with his wife and family in Bay Village, Ohio, "just a stone's throw from the Rock and Roll Hall of Fame and Museum, which is not a very smart thing to do since there's a lot of glass in that building."

MARSHA ROGERS is an educator in rural northern Nevada and is a founding member of the Shadow Canyon Writers in Hawthorne, Nevada.

ELAINE ROTHMAN, retired high school guidance counselor, writes essays and short fiction. She has recently completed her second novel, set in New York City in the 1930s and 1940s, which includes an expanded version of "This Night, Different from All Others."

SARA E. SANDERSON is an Indianapolis essayist, book reviewer, lecturer, and poet, having written commissioned lyrics for internationally performed music. A Meredith Fund, Texas, grant enabled her to travel to the Pacific Northwest, now often the setting of her poetry. Her work appeared in *Grow Old Along with Me—The Best Is Yet to Be* (Papier-Mache Press).

PAT SCHNEIDER is the author of five books, including *The Writer As an Artist: A New Approach to Writing Alone & with Others* (Lowell House) and *Wake Up Laughing: A Spiritual Autobiography* (Negative Capability Press). She is Director of Amherst Writers and Artists.

JAN EPTON SEALE lives in the Lower Rio Grande Valley of Texas where she writes and teaches writing. She writes short stories, essays, and poetry. Her work has appeared in two other Papier-Mache volumes.

DEBORAH SHOUSE says, "When I swim, I struggle to go underwater, to touch the rocky bottom. When I write, I face the same struggle: how to get deeper." Her work has appeared in *Newsweek, Ms.,* and *The Sun.* She is coauthor of *Working Woman's Communications Survival Guide.*

ANITA SKEEN is professor of English at Michigan State University where she teaches creative writing, Canadian literature, and women's studies. She is the author of two volumes of poetry, *Each Hand a Map* and *Portraits,* and is currently finishing another manuscript of poems, a collection of short stories, and a novel.

CLARENCE STILES graduated from high school in 1926 and taught in rural schools. He has worked as a linotype operator and printer, and was an operating engineer for the state of Illinois for thirty-two years prior to his retirement in 1981. He is a church elder emeritus, has been widowed since 1993, lives alone, drives his own car, gardens, cooks, writes, and travels.

CHRISTINE SWANBERG is the author of several books of poetry: *Tonight on This Late Road, Bread Upon the Waters, Slow Miracle, Invisible String,* and *The Tenderness of Memory*. She is the founder of the Rock River Poetry Prize, and publishes frequently in numerous journals. She performs poetry and music avidly and is a worldwide traveler and animal lover.

THERESE TAPPOUNI is a widely published poet, fiction writer, and mother of six. She thrives in Indian Shores, Florida. Therese writes and speaks about the strengths of women, and is working on a book concerning women's spiritual practice in today's world.

CINDA THOMPSON, grandchild to coal miners and union activists, was "born and raised" in Southern Illinois in a colorful locale known as Little Egypt. The life and times of the "inverted pyramid" between the mighty Mississippi and Ohio often filter into her work. An award-winning writer, Cinda is published in many anthologies and periodicals, among them Papier-Mache's *When I Am an Old Woman I Shall Wear Purple* and *The Tie That Binds*.

LORRAINE TOLLIVER is a professor of writing and literature at Compton Community College in Compton, California. She is a native of Kentucky. Her short stories and poems have appeared in *Poetry/LA, Writers International, Appalachian Heritage, College Journal, LA, Aim Quarterly, Contemporary Books,* and *The Tie That Binds* (Papier-Mache Press).

DAVI WALDERS is a poet and education consultant who delights that the same serious eaters have graced her Thanksgiving table in Maryland for twenty years. Her poems appear in such publications as *The American Scholar, Kalliope,* and *Ms.* and the recent Papier-Mache anthology, *Grow Old Along with Me—The Best Is Yet to Be.* She is the recipient of a 1997 Alden B. Dow Creativity Fellowship.

SUELLEN WEDMORE is a writer and a speech and language therapist who lives in Rockport, Massachusetts. She has been published in *Phoebe, Green Mountain Review,* and *I Am Becoming the Woman I've Wanted* (Papier-Mache Press). She is the mother of three grown children, and she lives with her physician husband in a Victorian house near the sea. Despite her complaints and protestations, she still considers Christmas her favorite holiday.

TONI WOOD is a writer whose articles have appeared in *Parents, Writer's Digest,* and *Baby Talk.* She is the author of a textbook, *Creative Activities for Children,* and a Kansas City-area guide for children called *WOW!* She and her husband live in Shawnee, Kansas, with their three boys.

In addition, the following Papier-Mache Staff members and their families submitted recipes to the collection: **SADIE BLOCK, JO GREGORY, JULIA GRISSOM, KELLY J. HUGHES, SHEILA KINKEAD, BARBARA KANTRO, SANDRA MARTZ, LORI VAN DYKE,** and **JOHNY VAN DYKE**. Special thanks to **JANICE BLOCK** for her assistance in obtaining recipes.

PAPIER-MACHE PRESS

At Papier-Mache Press, it is our goal to identify and successfully present important social issues through enduring works of beauty, grace, and strength. Through our work we hope to encourage empathy, respect, and communication among all people—young and old, male and female.

We appreciate you, our customer, and strive to earn your continued support. We also value the role of the bookseller in achieving our goals. We are especially grateful to the many independent booksellers whose presence ensure a continuing diversity of opinion, information, and literature in our communities. We encourage you to support these bookstores with your patronage.

We offer many beautiful books and gift items. Please ask your local bookstore or gift store which Papier-Mache items they carry. To obtain our complete catalog, mail your request to Papier-Mache Press, 627 Walker Street, Watsonville, CA 95076-4119; call our toll-free number, 800-927-5913; or e-mail your request to papierma@sprynet.com. You can also browse our complete catalog and writers' guidelines information on the web at http://www.ReadersNdex.com/papiermache.